The Bird Table Book
in Colour

The Bird Table Book in Colour

Tony Soper

illustrations by Robert Gillmor

David & Charles
Newton Abbot   London   North Pomfret (Vt)   Vancouver

By the same author:
The Wreck of the Torrey Canyon
(with Crispin Gill and Frank Booker)
Penguins (with John Sparks)
Owls (with John Sparks)
The Shell Book of Beachcombing
Wildlife Begins at Home
Everyday Birds

For Timothy Jan

ISBN 0 7153 7404 4
First Published October 1965
Reprinted November 1965
Reprinted December 1965
Second edition (revised) 1966
Third edition (revised) 1973
Reprinted 1974
Fourth edition (revised) 1977

Photoset in 11 on 12 Bembo
and printed and bound in Great Britain
by Redwood Burn Limited, Trowbridge & Esher
for David & Charles (Publishers) Limited
Brunel House Newton Abbot Devon

Published in the United States of America
by David & Charles Inc
North Pomfret Vermont 05053 USA

Published in Canada
by Douglas David & Charles Limited
1875 Welch Street North Vancouver BC

Contents

List of Illustrations

'Preparing the Food Tree'. Illustration from Martin Hiesemann's
book about The Theories of Baron von Berlepsch (1907)

Preface

Many crumbs have been eaten by many robins since this book was first launched twelve years ago. And interest in bird-gardening continues to grow, as my postman will confirm! So this new edition, much enhanced with fine colour photographs and with Robert Gillmor's illustrations blossoming into many hues, reflects the changing character of the bird-table scene. When the first *Bird Table Book* was written, no siskin had ever taken a peanut, so far as we know. Now they are two-a-penny on mesh baskets, joining reed buntings and lesser spotted woodpeckers, and also ring necked parrakeets and other exotic creatures.

It is clear that more species are learning to take advantage of bird tables and feeding stations. Just as well, when so much of their natural feeding ground is being swallowed up for unsympathetic development. All the more reason to try to create a house and garden which takes into account the requirements of wildlife as well as your own.

Feeding birds (and hedgehogs, badgers and toads, too) is a rewarding activity. Not only are these creatures good to see about the house, but their relationships with each other, with man, and with their surroundings, are of absorbing interest. So spare them an honest crust, with a bit of cheese as well.

1 The bird garden

Although the idea of living in a cave may seem to have its attractions, most of us inhabit a house. And in building ourselves a nest we inevitably disturb and deprive the previous 'owners', so it is good to feel that there are ways in which we may redress the balance. Gardens, and to a certain extent houses, provide the basic requirements of food and shelter for a whole community of wild plants and animals. As time goes by, more and more species are learning to visit garden feeding stations and take advantage of man's activities and generosity. In Devon, for instance, forty different species have taken food from a rural garden. Reed buntings, siskins and great spotted woodpeckers are examples of birds which are increasingly welcomed in suburban gardens in many parts of the British Isles. Exotic birds like the hoopoe, visiting southern England in the summer in increasing numbers, are as often as not seen in private gardens, enjoying the insect harvest of a well-kept lawn.

But while rarities are of interest, far and away the greatest pleasure of bird gardening is the year-in, year-out companionship of a group of individuals which have thrown in their lot with you and become residents. The swallows and housemartins of summer are a joy to welcome, but the robin which feeds from the hand and sings through the winter brings a deeper sense of community with his belonging.

An open well-kept lawn is almost essential to a bird garden. It gives a clear view and makes a happy hunting area for birds searching for ants, cockchafer

Waxwing (*Brian Hawkes/NHPA*)

grubs and worms. Worms are much misunderstood creatures and it is certainly a mistake to try to kill them off. They are useful; they aereate, drain and fertilise the soil, and though wormcasts may be unsightly they consist of fine rich soil. Spread them with a lawn rake or drag a weighted piece of wire netting over them before mowing. In the autumn, don't be too quick to sweep up the fallen leaves. Worms like leaves (especially willow and cherry), and birds like worms.

The bird garden should have a varied terrain, with changes of level, corners, miniature cliffs, valleys, hills, ravines, and low dry-stone walls – all features which will provide a diversity of insect life and rich foraging areas. Flower beds and neat borders do not offer much of interest, and an over-tidy garden is an unexciting hunting-ground. Try to organise a rock bank or low wall in a warm or south-facing part of the garden, so that it is less likely to be snowed up in winter. A reasonable amount of 'jungle', plenty of berry-bearing trees and shrubs, and a good lawn, are the important things to aim for.

If you've room for a patch of rough grass and nettles, please write them into your plan. A nettle-bed is highly productive of insects and will provide sustenance for many small birds. Cultivate the attitude of mind which sees a nettle-bed not as weeds but as a butterfly garden!

Incidentally, if you are having a new house built, be very careful that the builders set the topsoil aside for subsequent replacement before they start crashing about with bulldozers. Builders are all too ready to bury your vital topsoil under tons of useless subsoil, and you will find it is a long uphill grind to produce a fertile garden.

The best bird-garden boundary ever devised is the Devon hedgerow. A wide foundation-bank with rough stone and greenery, with ivy and ferns and wild flowers growing out of it, and topped with a close hawthorn or hazel hedge, is a bird paradise. One of the many beauties of a hedgerow is that it provides a variety of food in winter time when natural resources are at their lowest. Thrushes will eat berry-pulp and pass the pips. Then the finches and tits will eat the pips as they forage along the hedgerow bottom. Dead leaves and debris shelter hibernating flies and insects, spiders, woodlice and centipedes, all of which are good for wrens, tits, and dunnocks. In the hedge itself, the leaves stay attached and provide warmth and cover through the winter. The bank harbours yet more grubs and insects, wintering aphids, and their eggs, chrysalids, and so on. Common hedgerow birds are blackbird, thrush, chaffinch, yellow-hammer, dunnock, robin, wren, whitethroat, linnet, great tit, blue tit, long-tailed tit, and willow warbler. So one of the most distressing country sights is the bulldozing of hedgerows in order to make bigger fields.

If you haven't the space to develop a Devon hedgerow, then a thorn, holly or hazel hedge will do very well instead. Put a couple of crab-apple trees in it: they will provide useful stand-by food supplies in hard weather. Fieldfares will hack open the apples, and chaffinches will eat the pips.

Generally speaking, it is as well to avoid planting coarse thick-leaved evergreens. The rhododendrons and laurels beloved of town councils are unpromising bird habitats, taking light from the ground and not offering many insects in return. If you have lots of room then you might plant an isolated group of pine or larch in the hope of attracting goldcrests and crossbills. But have *some* evergreens, because they provide autumn and winter cover for roosting birds. A berry-bearing holly will serve a double purpose. Have one tall tree at least, a poplar for instance, and your thrush will sing from the topmost branch.

If you are lucky enough to have some old fruit trees, keep one or two for the birds. Leave the fruit on them and it will be welcomed by thrushes, fieldfares and redwings in the winter. Tits are also worth encouraging in orchards because they control the bug population. If you make sure there is a plentiful water supply, they may eat less of your fruit.

And when your trees die of old age, leave them to rot gently in peace, because in decay they are an important part of the woodland cycle. They provide food and shelter for yet more variety of species and, in principle, the greater the diversity of habitat you are able to offer, the healthier your garden will be. Those who scoff at gardens with nettle-beds and fungus-covered rotting tree trunks are simply displaying their ignorance of what life is all about! But if you want to 'improve' your rotting tree trunk, grow a climbing plant such as clematis to cover it.

In planting new trees, pick native rather than foreign species. Not only are they better adapted to the climate, but they are better integrated with the pattern of our flora and fauna. A mature oak or lime supports so much life that it is a complete community in itself, but of course it needs a great deal of space and time to reach maturity. So you may choose to plant quick-growing species like ash, elm, birch or willow. Remember that trees do not all have the same soil requirements. The easiest method of finding out what does well is to look around your neighbourhood, but a nurseryman will help.

Berry-bearing trees and shrubs

YEW. *Taxus baccata*. Evergreen. As a tree it may grow exceptionally to 90ft, but as a bush of only 6ft or so it makes a good hedge and provides nesting-sites. Slow growing, it may be fifteen years before it fruits and it may live for 2,000 years. A very good bird tree, the fleshy red berries are favourites with thrushes and starlings. The birds eat the pulp, but pass the poisonous seed without harm. Yew foliage and bark are also poisonous.

HAZEL. *Corylus avellana*. Deciduous bush, branching from the ground and growing to 15ft. Prefers rich soil, not too wet. Useful as hedgerow plant although it doesn't provide good nest sites (good pea sticks though). Nut harvest in August/September.

BARBARY (Common barbary). *Berberis vulgaris*. Deciduous. Grows thickly

13

Jay

Waxwing

Green
Woodpecker

Hoopoe

Rose-ringed
Parakeet

RG

2 Water

It is absolutely vital to provide a constant supply of clean water for your birds. Some can last a long time without drinking, some will die within a few days, but none can manage entirely without water for it is essential to the proper functioning of their bodies. Although birds do not sweat, they lose water, mainly by excretion, and must make up the loss. They will derive some water from their food, and the rest from drinking. Tree-living species may sip from foliage after rain, but most birds will visit ponds and streams. Some will fill their bills, then raise their heads to let the water run down their throats; some will keep their bills in the water; some will sip from the surface of the water as they fly past. Swifts and swallows even bathe in flight, dipping under with a quick splash as they go by.

Birds also need water to help with the continuing problem of keeping their plumage in order. Quite apart from the fact that feathers are a vital part of their flying apparatus, plumage acts as an insulator and regulates body temperature. To be fully efficient, the feathers must be kept in good condition, and feather maintenance looms large in a bird's life. Bathing is the first move in a complicated series of events.

The object of the bath is to wet the plumage without actually soaking it (if the feathers become too wet they may deteriorate). Birds will sometimes bathe in light rain, but if they are caught out in a heavy downpour they will hunch into a special position, reaching upwards and tightening their feathers so that the rain pours off quickly.

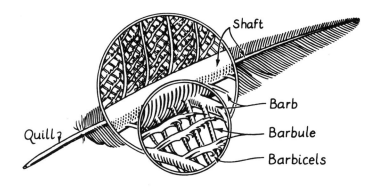

Shaft
Barb
Barbule
Barbicels
Quill?

After the bath the bird will shake itself and begin 'oiling'. With the tail twisted to one side, it will reach down with its bill to collect fatty oil from its preen gland. Then, very carefully, it will rub the oil into the feathers, all over the body. The difficult stage is when it wants to oil its head. To do this, it will use a foot, first oiling the foot and then scratching the grease onto the head. Next comes the preening session, when the bird will nibble and stroke all its feathers. This may take a long time, and afterwards the bird will stretch and settle itself until its plumage is in full flying and insulating order – all systems go.

Unless you are lucky enough to have a stream or pond in your garden you will obviously have to provide water in some form or another. The bird bath is the obvious answer, although it is not the best. However, if you are short of space, it will suffice. The simplest version is an upturned dustbin lid, supported by three bricks or sunk into the ground, although if you sink it, it will be more difficult to keep ice-free in winter. An advantage of keeping it off the ground is that you are providing extra foraging ground and possibly a toad-hole underneath! The water level should vary from about 1in depth to not more than 4in, and it should have a shallow approach as most birds prefer shallow water for bathing. Always use clean water and keep the bath up to its marks.

If you jib at introducing dustbin lids into your garden, use any similarly-shaped, shallow bowl, but beware of the ornamental, plastic, so-called 'bird baths' which garden shops sell and which may have a slippery slope leading to a cavernous well. The Rikden birdbath does the job very well (see page 105 for supplier). Whatever kind of bowl you use, put it in shade and within reasonable range of cover and safety, but not so close that a cat may lurk and pounce. A point to remember is that birds get rather excited and preoccupied about their bathing; they tend, therefore, to be more vulnerable then than at other times.

Robin bathing (*John Markham/Bruce Coleman Ltd*)

Sketches of a
young Robin
preening
after bathing

and cleared, introduce some fish. Goldfish if you like, but why not stick to good British species like sticklebacks and minnows? Any of these will deal with the mosquito and gnat larvae which will try to colonise the pond. But don't overstock. A rough rule of thumb is that each inch of fish requires 24 sq in of surface area.

Water snails will graze the encroaching algae, but don't have too many. One snail to every 1–2 sq ft of surface water is the rule. Ramshorn (*Planorbis corneus*) or freshwater winkles (*Paludina vivipara*) are probably the best species, least likely to damage your plants.

There are plenty of other creatures you can introduce, such as newts, frogs, water-spiders and beetles (but be sparing with great diving beetles – *Dytiscus marginalis* – because they are fierce and will attack fish much bigger than themselves). You will find that the finished product will give you as much pond-watching pleasure as it does the birds and if, one day, a heron comes and eats your fish you must grin and bear it and re-stock the pond.

It really isn't possible, or natural, to try to run a sort of 'paradise garden' in which predators have no place. However hard it may be for us to reconcile ourselves to it, the fact is that predators, like foxes, sparrowhawks and herons, which prey on and eat other species, are operating in the best interests of the species on which they prey. By catching the slower individuals which are off colour or sick, they are continually weeding out the less healthy members of a species so that it is the fittest which survive. So please do try to understand both sides of the argument. When the magpie eats eggs or small birds it is doing its job as a magpie, not acting like a pantomime villain!

Unless your garden is on sandy ground, you may like to provide a dust bath for sparrows and wrens. The dusting-place should be well sheltered, with some cover nearby, and can consist of a couple of square feet of well-sifted sand, earth and ash to a depth of a few inches. Sprinkle the dust bath with bug powder or spray (eg Cooper's Household Insect Powder or Poultry Aerosol) every now and again, for the common good. Birds will also sun-bathe, smoke-bathe, and even bathe in ants, all strange manifestations of the need to maintain feather performance at peak efficiency.

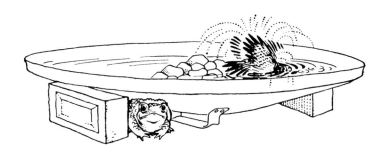

Blue tits (*E. A. Janes*)

(*Jeffrey Taylor*)

3 Nest sites and nestboxes

When your garden is stocked with welcoming berry-laden shrubs and a drinking pool, the next move is to induce some of your bird visitors to go the whole hog and take up permanent residence. By their nature houses, outbuildings and gardens provide dozens of potential nest sites, although in these tidy-minded days we tend to build with fewer holes and corners. Very often, we can turn an uninviting building into a highly-desirable bird residence with the minimum of effort. Once again, we must bear in mind that different birds have different requirements, and while a blue tit will choose a secret place, entered by what seems an impossibly narrow hole, a swan will build a great mound of a nest and sit in state for all to see. In many coastal areas we have the curious spectacle of herring gulls choosing to nest on rooftops and by chimney pots.

We can divide birds roughly into those which nest in holes and those which do not. Tits, nuthatches, tree-sparrows, redstarts and woodpeckers are hole-nesters, while spotted flycatchers, robins, blackbirds and thrushes live mostly on the open plan. All birds, no matter what type of nest they choose, need protection from their enemies and shelter from the elements if they are to thrive, so most of them build in cover of some kind.

Natural nest sites

Hedges are the most obvious places for nests. A good beech, holly, hawthorn or yew hedge contains dozens of likely building-sites and also provides a good defence barrier. It is important that there should be plenty of forks in the branches to provide a foundation for the first nest twigs. (Hazel makes a poor nesting tree because it offers so few fork sites.) By judicious pruning at about the 5ft height you can often turn an unpromising hedge into a likely attraction. Prune your hedge in early spring and autumn, leaving it undisturbed during the breeding season. When pruning fruit trees, make a crotch-site here and there in the body of the tree, in the hope of attracting a goldfinch to nest.

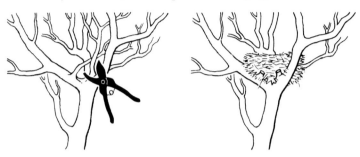

The berry-bearing shrubs often serve as nesting areas in the spring; if you have brambles and gorse in your garden, you may find they will harbour dunnocks or linnets. Honeysuckle seems to have a special attraction for flycatchers. Once a bird has chosen its nest site leave it to get on with the job. Don't try to help it with the construction, and don't 'improve' the situation, or it may desert. Don't fuss it!

A friend of mine who made an island on his pond was rewarded by having a pair of Canada geese take it over. If you are lucky enough to have plenty of water, grow a lush area of wild celery, millet, reeds and sedges in clumps. If the reed-bed is large enough, you may get reed and sedge warblers, and possibly reed buntings, building in it.

Now for the hole-nesters. Naturally, they will prefer tree holes and it may be that you already have some old trees – fruit trees, perhaps – which have begun to decay in a manner attractive to birds. If not, you might consider introducing some holes into a decaying tree with a brace and bit. Start some promising holes of about 1¼in diameter and a woodpecker may finish the job. If the woodpecker gives up, a nuthatch may take over and plaster the entrance hole with mud to suit its own preference. Or, you might try importing an old tree or tree trunk, complete with holes, and setting it up in a secluded position. At worst, you will end up with a pair of starlings. Personally, I like to have a pair of starlings nesting nearby because they are such entertaining vocalists and are remarkable mimics. We once had one that gave a first-class rendering of a hen that had just laid an egg, but the climax of its repertoire was a beautiful pussy-cat's miaow.

Making and enlarging holes is great fun, and when you have finished working on trees, you might turn your attentions to the walls of your house and outbuildings. Quite often it is possible to enlarge cracks so that there is the $1\frac{1}{8}$in necessary for a tit to squeeze through. I am not suggesting you tear your house apart just for a few birds, but you will find plenty of likely and safe places if you look around, armed with a strong auger or jemmy. Try drilling some discreet $1\frac{1}{8}$in holes in your garage doors. Make one entrance up near the roof and swallows may colonise the loft, although you will need to have a ceiling to protect the cellulose of your car from the droppings.

If you are building a garden wall, do not overdo the pointing; leave one or two gaps and you may attract a pied wagtail. Even grey wagtails take freely to man-provided nest sites in culvert and bridge stone-work. The height of the holes and cavities is not vitally important, although round about the 5ft mark is probably ideal. With a desirable site, birds will not be too choosy. Robins have nested at ground level and great tits as high as 24ft, although these are exceptional instances. The holes should, however, be in a sheltered position and facing somewhere within an arc drawn from north through east to south-east. Hot sun is bad, and so is an entrance facing into a cold wind. Heat, especially, can easily kill young nestlings when they become exhausted.

An ancient, disintegrating stone wall is an asset to cherish and so is an old garden shed. The wall may be a haven for tits, nuthatches and wagtails, and the shed may be a thriving bird slum in no time at all if you develop it a little. Shelves around the walls and under the roof at different heights could provide homes for swallows, blackbirds and robins. A bundle of pea sticks in a corner may make a home for a wren. Leave an old tweed coat hanging up with a wide pocket gaping open for a robin. Keep the floor clear, though, to discourage rats. If necessary, put a rat-trap tunnel against the walls, but see that it does not let in light and attract ground birds. Make sure there is a good entrance hole somewhere, in case a bird is locked in by mistake.

On the outside of the shed grow a jungle of creeping ivy and honeysuckle, for it may well entice a robin to build. Hide a half-coconut (with a drain-hole in the bottom of the cup) in the creeper for a possible spotted flycatcher. Try excavating a nest cavity in the middle of a brushwood bundle and lean it against an outside wall. Lastly, lean an old plank against the dampest, darkest wall to make a haven for snails, and farm them on behalf of the thrushes.

Man-made nest sites

There is good historical precedent for putting up bird houses (Noah had a dove-cote on top of the Ark). In Roman times there was a thriving pigeon 'fancy' with rooftop pigeon towns. Columbaria of differing architectural styles spread from Rome through Europe to Scotland and the rest of Britain through the centuries. The custom declined in the eighteenth century, when the introduction of root and clover crops made it possible to keep more cattle and sheep through the winter, thus providing fresh meat which made the pigeon 'squab' redundant.

Herring gull at Brixham (*Tony Soper*)

Blackbird family at home (*Walter Murray/NHPA*)

Wren at nest (*D. N. Dalton/NHPA*)

In the Middle Ages clay flasks and wooden boxes were used to attract small birds to nest, in order that the resulting fat juveniles could be taken for food. Probably the first man to use nestboxes simply for the pleasure of encouraging birds to nest was the eccentric Yorkshire naturalist Charles Waterton, in the early nineteenth century.

But the traditional back-garden nestbox is the robin's kettle, stuck 5ft up in the fork of a tree. The kettle should be at least quart size, and the spout should point down so that rainwater can drain away. As an encouragement, prime the nest with some dead leaves or a plaited circle of straw.

The most unusual man-made nest site I ever saw was a birdcage, hanging high up on a cob wall in the village of Middle Wallop in Hampshire. It turned out that a hoopoe had reared young in a perfectly normal cavity-site in the wall, but one of the nestlings had fallen out of the hole a bit too soon. The villagers had hoisted up the birdcage and left the door open, installing the unfortunate young bird inside. Incredibly, the adult hoopoe carried on feeding the baby as if nothing had happened, going in and out of the birdcage as if it were the most ordinary thing in the world. The story has a happy ending, too, because the whole family finally fledged successfully and flew off. But hoopoes are rare breeders in this country, so I am not going to suggest that we all invest in hoopoe birdcages.

Every year for some time past a pair of mute swans has tried to nest on a tidal sandbank near the mouth of the estuary at Newton Ferrers in South Devon. They seem unable to grasp the fact that Atlantic seawater rises and falls, and as fast as they build a nest the rising tide washes it away. The scientists of the International Paint Company, who have a research station nearby, came to the rescue, constructing a special swan raft on empty 5gal oil drums. They anchored it in position and piled the beginning of a swan's nest onto it. The swans took it over and now every year they complete their nest, lay eggs, brood and hatch the cygnets; every time the tide comes in, the nest and contents rise gently and float, serene and safe.

Rafts have also been used successfully to encourage wild ducks, great-crested grebes, common terns, greylag and Canada geese, moorhens and coots. Their great advantage is that they give a degree of safety from land-borne predators, but they are easier to write about than to construct. They consist of a platform supported by buoyancy tanks, 40gal drums or steel tanks, held by a framework of timber or angle iron. The platform, or deck, should be devised to carry a layer of soil or shingle stabilised with suitable plants, polythene sheeting will help to retain sufficient rain water to keep the soil wet. Make sure that there is a ramp or some sort of suitable access point so that the birds can launch themselves into the water and get back onto the raft easily.

In the Dee estuary, common terns have successfully colonised a raft moored on a reservoir belonging to the British Steel Corporation. The raft, constructed by the Merseyside Ringing Group, was a massive affair of telegraph poles

28

decked with railway sleepers, covered with slag, shingle and grass sods. Blocks of expanded polystyrene provided the buoyancy and the resulting 'floating island' was 100sq ft, taking the weight of three men with ease. Secured by nylon lines to scrap iron anchors, this incongruous device floated serenely in a scene characterised by slag tips, blast furnaces, power stations, and the constant disturbance of a modern steel works. Yet the terns arriving in spring from their West African wintering grounds took up residence and successfully defended their new territory against the attentions of herring gulls.

As the months went by a colony of terns became established, and in that first year the Merseyside group ringed sixteen young birds. In this way, what had been a steady decline in numbers at the nearby old-established ternery was halted, and it is hoped that the Dee tern colony will soon be up to its former strength. A fine example of the way in which intelligent interpretation of a species' needs may help to maintain it in adverse conditions.

All over Europe there are traditions which have led people to encourage birds to adopt man-made nest sites. In many villages in Germany, a cartwheel is fixed to the top of a high pole in the hope of attracting a stork to nest. And in Switzerland and Holland they have developed a successful pole-top nestbox for kestrels. If you have a large secluded garden in good kestrel country (and this includes some cities), you might consider the experiment of putting up one of these boxes. Farmers who are bothered with mice might also think it worth the effort. (Constructional details are given on page 66.) Kestrels are among those species which are learning to take advantage of the urban life. In 1971 a kestrel family successfully used a window box on the sixteenth floor of a 20-storey block of flats at Peckham, London. Two chicks were fledged on a diet of house sparrows. The owner of the flat found the birds too messy for her comfort, and boarded up the ledge, but the hawks were undismayed, nesting successfully the following year on the nearest suitable tower block, in Southwark.

There are two basic types of nestbox: an enclosed space with a small entrance hole, and a tray or ledge with or without sides and roof. They can be readily obtained at reasonable prices (suppliers' addresses are given on page 105) or you may prefer to make your own; there is an extra satisfaction in seeing birds

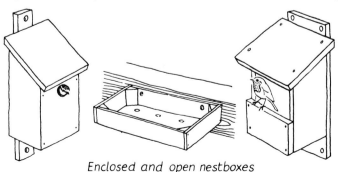

Enclosed and open nestboxes

Robin with food for nestlings (*Eric Hosking*)

Pied flycatcher (*Eric Hosking*)

Spotted flycatcher (*Brian Hawkes/NHPA*)

Farmhouse dovecote, south-west France (*Tony Soper*)

take over a nestbox you have built with your own hands. The method of construction will be discussed here in general terms, as the type of box and critical sizes for each species will be found listed in the notes in Chapter 6. The nest-hole measurement most people want to know straightaway is one which excludes starlings and sparrows. The answer is 1⅛in. This will give entry to all the tits, and nuthatches, but also tree sparrows, which may not be quite so welcome. Starlings cannot manage a hole smaller than 1½in diameter, and house sparrows are deterred by holes under 1¼in. But they have a disconcerting habit of trying hard even if they can't get in, and may prevent other species gaining access simply by laying claim to the site and poking nest material into the hole. The hole-type of nestbox is usually the most successful, because it reproduces the type of nest site which is harder to find round the average house. And also because suburban birds tend to be woodland species which are largely hole-in-tree nesters.

But remember that blackbirds, pied wagtails and robins, for instance, live on the 'open plan' and need a very large entrance. So make boxes of both types.

Although at first sight it may seem that the 'rustic' type of nestbox will be most suitable I think the plain kind is preferable; the birds certainly do not seem to mind one way or the other, so the main criteria are construction and amenity. The plain square types are undoubtedly easiest to make, and I think they look most attractive. The 'rustic' boxes are usually made of birch. If they were only fixed to birch trees I should have no objection, but this is seldom the case. Birch boxes attached to oak or beech or elm trees make rather an unhappy and unnatural contrast. Perhaps there is some case for using rustic boxes when it is important that they should not be too easily discovered, in public places for instance, but I think it is a weak one. Small boys on the warpath will discover either type in no time, and if this is a danger the boxes should be fixed high, say not less than 12ft.

The boxes should be made of ¾in wood, which will stand up to weathering for a reasonable time and be thick enough to insulate the interior temperature from violent changes. Hardwood is most suitable as it is more resistant to weather than softwood. Seasoned oak is probably the best, although it is hard to cut and may split. Of the softwoods, cedar is very satisfactory and weathers well. Second-hand floor boarding serves well, and is often exactly the right size for the job. You can get it, sometimes for the asking, from any building site where they are renovating old houses.

It is important that the box should not warp and so allow wind and rain to attack the nestlings. One side may be removable for cleaning purposes, but make sure that it fits firmly in position when in use and that there is no danger of it falling out and exposing the nest to predators. Make sure that the roof fits flush to the walls so that the box is as watertight as possible, and also that the roof overlaps the outside edges so that rain drips clear.

Seal the wall joints with a sealing compound, such as Seelastic or Bostik,

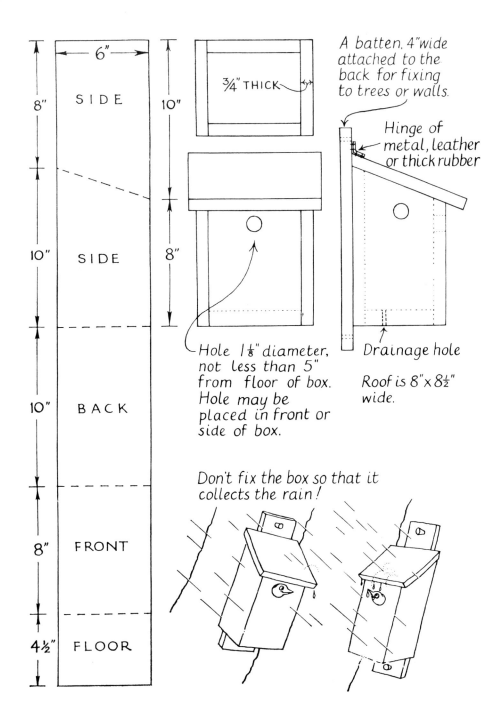

8"

6"

SIDE

10"

SIDE

10"

BACK

8"

FRONT

4½"

FLOOR

10"

¾" THICK

8"

A batten, 4"wide attached to the back for fixing to trees or walls.

Hinge of metal, leather or thick rubber

Hole 1⅛" diameter, not less than 5" from floor of box. Hole may be placed in front or side of box.

Drainage hole

Roof is 8" x 8½" wide.

Don't fix the box so that it collects the rain!

before you finally nail or screw the pieces into position. Rain kills many nest-lings in natural nest sites and we should take particular care to exclude it when we invite birds to use the boxes we provide. The entrance hole should be at the top of the box, otherwise a cat may be able to fish the young birds out, or they may be seen by other predators when they stretch up to beg for food. The inside floor measurements must allow birds plenty of room to stretch their growing wings. Make a ventilation and drainage hole in the floor, since some birds are not too particular about their nest sanitation. The better you make the box the more important is the drain hole. This is one form of carpentry where the bad workman very often produces the most suitable result.

It isn't necessary to paint the finished box, but a coat of creosote will increase its probable life-span. *Audubon Magazine*, in the United States, reported an eleven-year study in which a whole range of coloured nestboxes was offered to birds, in order to see if they had preferences. Of 98 used boxes, 41 were red, 31 green, 16 blue, 8 yellow, 2 white. They don't seem to have offered black ones, which would probably have been unpopular, and it is a pity they didn't offer natural wood and creosoted wood for comparison. Anyway, it's clear that you should avoid yellow or white! If you *change* colour, birds will take a little time to accept that change, because it induces a 'scared' response similar to that pro-duced by a predator.

Ideally the nestboxes should be fixed in position in October or November. This gives them a chance to weather into their surroundings, and their potential occupiers have plenty of time to get used to them and to explore their possibilities. It may well be that they will be used during the winter months as a roost box. There is an astonishing account, by experienced nestbox watchers in Norfolk, of a box with an interior space of $4\frac{1}{2} \times 5\frac{1}{2} \times 5\frac{3}{4}$in being occupied at night by over sixty wrens, huddled together for winter warmth and occupying 2.33 cubic inches per body!

Nestboxes may, of course, be put up at any time in the winter, but if you are hoping they will be occupied in their first spring, they ought to be up by the end of February. However, better late than never, especially if there's a shor-tage of natural sites.

The boxes can be fixed at about the 6ft level, though the height is not the

most important factor. The position should be protected from prevailing cold winds and shaded from the hot sun: as already mentioned, the box should face somewhere in the arc from north through east to south-east. The location should not be thickly sheltered or darkened by foliage, and the adult birds should have a fairly clear flight path to and from the nest. A convenient staging post should be available, some 6ft away.

The entrance hole must be far enough from its fixing wall or tree trunk to allow the incoming bird to have fully-stretched wings till the last moment before landing. Don't have a landing perch attached to the box, as this may provide a cat or a squirrel with a good position for extracting the babies. Your birds certainly don't need the perch to help them enter the box. If you want a

Great tit (*E. Breeze-Jones/Bruce Coleman Ltd*)

perch for photographic purposes put it several feet away. The birds will probably be glad to use it as a staging-post.

The box should be fixed in such a way that the top of the entrance hole wall is inclined outwards to exclude rain, and it should be secured to its anchorage by means of a batten, so that it does not become waterlogged where attached to the wall or trunk. It is not important to fix the box firmly although obviously it is good sense, since it is vital that it doesn't fall down. From the bird's point of view, a box which swings in the wind is no more than the artificial version of a swaying branch. Use copper nails when fixing the box to a tree, if there is any chance that the tree may be subsequently felled for timber. It will be kinder to the saw blade.

Do not put up too many boxes too close together: Like some of us, some birds prefer to keep their distance from each other (although this does not apply to colonial nesters like martins). Many species with a strong territorial instinct like to 'own' their plot but, fortunately, they do not as a rule object to members of other species living nearby. Thus robins, which have a highly-developed sense of territory, will not object to tits as close neighbours. It is difficult to say how many boxes should be erected because so many factors are involved, but where there is a large area to cover it is probably worth trying a dozen to the acre; more if the area is drastically short of natural nest sites. Put up twice as many enclosed boxes as open ones. If there are good natural or semi-natural sites available it may be that the boxes will be ignored altogether. On the other hand, blue tits may inspect, 'buy' and start building within a day of erection.

Open plan boxes should be fixed in suitable crotch-sites in trees and bushes, and cunningly hidden in ivy or creeper-clad walls. However cleverly you may hide them away you can be quite certain the birds will find them without any delay.

One more thing will help make your boxes attractive. Put a shallow layer of moss, or thin plaited straw, in the bottom of boxes destined for passerines. If you are hoping for a woodpecker, try priming the box with a sprinkling of sawdust or chippings and, as an appetizer, a few beetles and grubs. In early spring, when the birds are beginning to build, they will be searching everywhere for nesting materials. Jackdaws will take paper bags from litter-bins, or perch on a horse's back to steal hairs. When I was on the Galápagos Islands I once found a cormorant's nest that had a boat's rowlock ingeniously woven into the structure.

Birds are more than willing to be helped with their search for construction materials. Straw, feathers, dog or cat combings, short bits of cotton, cotton wool, sheep wool and poultry down (after treatment with bug-powder) are all grist of their mill. Stuff them in two mesh bags – hanging one from the bird table or branch and pegging the other to the ground for ground-birds. There is nothing more charming than a sitting bird surrounded by a delicate garnish of coloured cottons. A naturalist once took a sparrow's nest to pieces and found it consisted of 1,282 separate items, which included 1,063 pieces of dead grass, 126 strips of bark, 15 pieces of paper, 10 pieces of cellophane, 13 pieces of tissue, 25 pieces of cotton thread, 28 wild bird feathers, one piece of string and a cotton bandage. The disadvantage of these exhibitionist nests is that they are somewhat conspicuous, and may attract predators.

Woodpeckers or sparrows may 'improve' a nestbox, and in one case a squirrel was reported to have enlarged a small hole to 2½in diameter. Having gained entrance, the intruder may well eat the young chicks it finds inside. To foil this activity, the RSPB make a metal plate, with a tit-size hole in it, which can be fixed over the vulnerable wood. But even a vandalised box may produce happy results, for a nuthatch may come along and plaster the edges of the hole to suit its own requirements.

Both great and blue tits will sometimes peck at the entrance holes to their boxes, but this is perfectly normal behaviour; it is not their way of telling you that the hole is too small.

Never alter the position of a box after a bird has adopted it, and never disturb the bird when it is sitting. You will often hear people speak of the tameness of sitting birds; the truth is that the brooding instinct is stronger than the bird's terror of being close to a human. The privacy of a bird's nest should be respected and we should neither fuss nor photograph without good reason.

And when, at last, your nestbox contains a noisy, struggling muddle of baby birds, try to contain yourself and do not peer in too often. Examine the box every two or three days, and only when the adult bird is not at home. Nothing disconcerts a wild bird quite so much as the sudden appearance of a vast human face 3in away from it. Be particularly careful not to cause nearly-fledged birds to leave the nest too soon. This is a critical time, and it would be a disaster if the brood 'exploded' into the world before their time. If you inadvertently cause the young birds to fly, collect them up carefully and 'post' them back into the box. Stuff the entrance hole with a handkerchief for ten minutes or so. And then when the panic has subsided, remove the handkerchief very, very gently.

All birds are attacked by parasites such as fleas, lice and bird flies, so after the young have flown from the box it should be cleaned out and given a dose of a pyrethrum-based bug killer, eg Cooper's Poultry Aerosol. Do not use DDT. If you now prime the deloused box with a thin layer of moss it will, perhaps, serve for a second brood or be ready later on for use as a winter roost box.

Incidentally, don't worry if when you come to clean out your box you find one or two eggs that did not hatch, or even one or two dead young. This is a common enough occurrence, possibly due to a shortage of food at a critical time, but it is part of the natural course of events. If every blue tit egg developed into an adult blue tit, there very soon wouldn't be room on planet earth for any of the rest of us.

Nuthatch feeding nestling (*Robert Burton/Bruce Coleman Ltd*)

Blue tits inside nestbox (*OSF/Bruce Coleman Ltd*)

Much of the ornithologist's knowledge and understanding of the various stages of the breeding cycle in hole-nesting birds comes from nestbox studies. The British Trust for Ornithology has for years been recording nestbox information on special cards, which are subsequently analysed in computer fashion, but they are careful to insist that the interests of the birds comes before the importance of the card. If you would like to join in with this important work, contact the BTO (see address page 112). And you will certainly want to get hold of the Trust's excellent field guide, *Nestboxes*, by J. J. M. Flegg and D. E. Glue. It is the definitive book on nestboxes and was written for research workers who use them for bird breeding studies.

4 The bird table

Housed in comfort and surrounded by a garden which provides them with worms, berries and fresh water, your birds have little to complain about. But if you are prepared to go one step further, you can give yourself a great deal of extra pleasure. By providing food you can entice the birds to show themselves more freely in places where you can watch them. And, as the availability of food controls to some extent the bird population of your garden, you will also be increasing their numbers. But providing food is not a pleasure to undertake lightly. Put out some scraps in the garden and you will very soon attract new residents. They will become dependent on your generosity, and if it fails they will be competing for an inadequate supply of natural foods. Especially in cold weather birds may lose a lot of weight overnight, and they have to make it up again during the brief hours of daylight. Death comes in a matter of hours even to a healthy small bird, if it is without food. In hard weather the real killer is hunger, not cold.

The problems are simple enough to list: what to provide, and how to serve it? You may think it sufficient simply to throw bread scraps onto the lawn, but this will not do at all. Bread alone, especially mass-produced white bread, is about as good for birds as it is for us, and certainly does not constitute a satisfactory diet. Besides, some birds do not care to come down to ground level for their food; in any case there is always the threat of a cat waiting in the wings! Again some birds are carnivorous and others vegetarian. It is no good offering

House Sparrow

Wren

Dunnock

Chaffinch

Robin

a snail to a chaffinch, or a sunflower seed to a wren. A quick glance at a bird's bill will give a clue to its diet. Finches have nutcracker bills, adapted to crack and crush, and they feed mostly on grain and seeds. They are hard-billed birds. In the other basic category, soft-bills, we have, for instance, robins and wrens with slender bills adapted to deal with grubs, caterpillars and other insects.

Natural food

The best food to provide is what the birds would choose for themselves. One way to do this is to go on a nut and berry collecting expedition in the autumn. From August to October, you will be able to collect a fine harvest along the hedgerows. Pick the berries when they are just ripe.

In August your target should be the rowan. Later on, elderberries are first-quality bird food. Rowan and elder are probably the best berries, but wild cherry and haws are also good. Sloes do not seem to be very much liked by birds, nor are blackberries very popular. Crab-apples are worth collecting, and in a bad winter you will find fieldfares coming to the bird table for them. As for nuts, the best choice is the hazel, but almonds are also very useful, especially for pleasing great spotted woodpeckers. Collect conkers and sweet chestnuts, acorns and beech-mast from the ground as soon as they have fallen.

Dry the berries, and store both berries and nuts in a dry, dark place, and they will keep until you need them. Use shallow trays and arrange the fruits in a single layer. Gather pine and larch cones and take out the seeds from between the woody scales. Store all seeds, including weed-seeds such as thistle, knap-weed, teazle, ragwort and stinging-nettle, in muslin bags, hung up where the air can get at them. In severe weather when the ground is hard with frost, take a spade and turn some earth over. This will provide a much-needed supplement to the bird table food.

Kitchen scraps

Many people will tell you that birds love bread, and though this is true, nobody would suggest that bread alone provides a balanced diet. It is better than nothing and wholemeal is better than white, but it is a poor substitute for a varied selection of more nutritious food. One of my correspondents, Mrs Elizabeth Hughes of Bexley in Kent, says that the most popular bird table food in her garden is uncooked pastry, which her blue tits prefer even to cheese, chopped bacon rinds and boiled ham skin. One of the advantages of this food is that it can be moulded into all sorts of odd cracks and crannies round the bird table.

Potato, especially baked in the jacket, is a useful staple. Stale cake is good, especially if home made with a high protein content. Minced raw meat, meat bones, cooked and chopped bacon rinds and cheese are all good. An excellent use for fat is as a binding material for bird-pudding – the best kitchen scrap bird offering of all, for which some recipes are given on page 104. Almost everything except highly-seasoned or salty food can go into the basket for bird kitchen scraps. Be careful to exclude salt though, for it will kill most small birds. But on the whole you don't need to worry about giving birds something that may disagree with them; they will select what suits them and leave the rest. One way and another, you will not find much is wasted.

And, if you have one of those splendid whole Stilton cheeses at Christmas, don't throw away the near-empty shell when it is finished. Birds are very partial to Stilton, but prefer it when it is not swamped with port! Melon seeds can be another exotic bird table success.

Specially-bought food

There are several firms producing bird food (see list on page 104) and, if you can stand the expense, this is certainly an easy way to solve the supply problem. John Haith Ltd, of Cleethorpes, for instance, produce a 'wild bird food' which caters for most tastes. With mixed seeds, especially sunflower seeds, and peanut kernels, your birds will be well served.

Peanuts are, without a doubt, a 'best buy'. They are full of calories, convenient to handle, store and serve. Unshelled, they can be strung up to serve as playthings for tits and nuthatches. Other nuts are all worth buying. Nuthatches, in particular, love brazils. Coconut is good, but serve it in shell, (sawn in half and suspended so that rain can't get in) not desiccated or ground, as this will swell up inside a bird's stomach with dire results. It is especially important not to offer ground coconut in the breeding season, when it may be fed too generously to juvenile tits. Generally speaking, there should be enough natural food available for birds during the late spring and summer, and it is unwise to feed freely, if at all. Peanuts, for instance, cannot be digested by young nestling tits. I don't know whether coconut juice is good for birds, but you might like to experiment. Starlings love milk, and so do tits.

Mixed wild-bird seed can be bought from pet shops. But the most welcome seed, which nuthatches love, is hemp. Split some for the smaller birds, or buy it in crushed form. Sunflower, canary, millet, maize, oats, and corn are all good. Coarse oatmeal from chain-stores, should be offered raw, as porridge is too glutinous and sticks to plumage and bill. Rice, on the other hand, should be boiled before you serve it.

You may be able to arrange with your local fruiterer for a box of unsaleable fruit to be kept aside for you. Apples, oranges, tomatoes, grapefruit, bananas and grapes are all equally acceptable if you just cut them up. In hard times, birds will eat this fruit ravenously, and in very cold weather suet may usefully be added because it provides energy so efficiently. Great spotted woodpeckers are especially fond of suet, which you can cram into the odd cranny.

For live insect food, the best buys are mealworms and ants' eggs. Robins are mad about mealworms. You can buy them direct from pet shops or bird-food suppliers, or you can breed them yourself. (Addresses on page 104.) Serve the mealworms in a fairly deep, round dish, so that they cannot escape – they are surprisingly mobile. Gentles are sometimes recommended, but, though I have not tasted them myself, I think they are rather indigestible and a poor substitute for mealworms. They are cheaper than mealworms, but nastier, and they should never be offered during the breeding season, as they are quite unsuitable for nestlings. Ants' eggs (ant pupae) can be collected from under stones in your garden; it is rather hard work for small return but the birds will be grateful. And always put the stone back in place so as not to upset the other creatures whose roof it is.

Birds not only have varying food requirements, both in nature and at the bird table, but they also have varying methods of hunting. Some skulk about on the ground, some snoop along branches and foliage, and some run about on tree trunks and stone walls. So we must have variety of presentation as well as variety of food.

Bird tables

The traditional way of feeding is with a bird table and, although it has limitations, it is on the whole a very satisfactory method. The table can either be supported on a post or it can hang from the bough of a tree, or a bracket. Your own situation will probably decide the method you use. There is little to choose between the two systems so long as you keep the cat problem firmly in mind and do not fix the hanging model to a potential cat-way. The feeding tray should not be too small. Somewhere between the 2–4sq ft mark is ideal. Put a coaming round the edge to stop the food being blown off, but leave a gap in it somewhere so that the table can be cleared and cleaned easily, and water can run off.

Whether it hangs or stands on a pedestal or post, the tray should be about 5–6ft off the ground. The safest post is a piece of galvanised iron tubing, but any smooth pole will do, as long as you get it firmly into the ground. The most unsuitable support is one of those awful 'rustic' things that positively invite squirrels and cats to climb up to their burglarious work. The table should be in a position where it gets neither too much sun nor too much cold wind. It should be within reasonable distance – say, a couple of yards – of cover, but out of cat-jumping range. The point is that the woodland species, like blue tits, which frequent gardens, are not keen on a long flight over open ground to get to the table. Showing themselves too freely in the open makes them vulnerable to predators. Arrange things so that they can reach the haven of your bird table by way of short spurts between bushes, or sheds, or staging posts of some kind. If the terrain is open, provide hazel sticks at regular intervals. You'll soon learn the birds' requirements, and see how they like to survey a situation before exposing themselves. The bird table does not need a roof but it is an advantage. A roof keeps the food drier, provides a place for a hanging seed-hopper, and may even be used as a roosting place at night. Birds will often use a covered bird table to shelter from a shower of rain. If the table has a roof-hopper, this should be kept full of mixed seed for the finches. On the tray, you can distribute your main offering of scraps and bird-pudding. Ideally, the food should be in pieces either so big that birds cannot carry it away, or so small that they do not want to carry it away: medium-sized bits tend to find their way to the nearest bush, where they get lost and encourage rats and mice. Another solution to this problem is to make a removable, close-mesh, wire-netting frame which fits inside the coaming, covers the food, and prevents big birds flying off with large lumps.

A particularly fine type of bird table is used by my friend, E. H. Ware. He has rehabilitated the bottom part of a blown-down apple tree, cutting the trunk off just above the roots, and cutting the branches a couple of feet above the fork. With a tray fixed across the fork, and coconuts, feeders and suet-bag hanging from the ends of the branches, he has a good-looking and versatile feeding station. Another of its advantages is that it provides 'queuing space' for birds to wait their opportunity while a bully is monopolising the tray.

Perhaps the most unusual of all bird tables is that provided by the Royal Navy. The RN Birdwatching Society has a 'Feed the Birds' campaign in

Blue tit (*John Markham/Bruce Coleman Ltd*)

Great tit (*Walter Murray/NHPA*)

Robins like mealworms (*John Markham/Bruce Coleman Ltd*)

The feeding tray should not be too small - around three or four square feet is ideal. A coaming stops food blowing off.

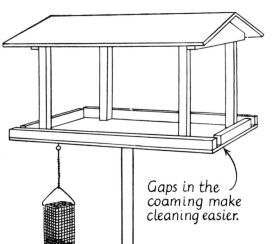

The R.S.P.B. table (above) is complete with chains for hanging and an adaptor for fitting to a post.

A food hopper is shown fitted under the roof.

Gaps in the coaming make cleaning easier.

A food basket for scraps or nuts is very popular with tits.

A galvanised tube or smooth pole is ideal.

About five or six feet high.

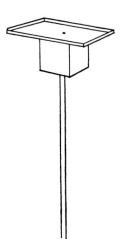

A biscuit tin fixed under the table is a useful anti-squirrel device.

which three vessels are experimenting with different feeds, provided for land birds on migration and far from home. These birds very often get relief from their exhaustion by resting on ships at sea. For instance, two female kestrels were fed with raw steak, and a racing pigeon did well on sweetcorn and peanuts. High in arctic latitudes, a brambling and two snow buntings were successfully fed on 'Swoop', and continued their journeys.

Scrap baskets

The advantage of scrap baskets is that the food is less likely to get blown about and scattered. The disadvantage is that thrushes and blackbirds cannot manage to hang on to them when they are suspended. The simplest scrap container is one of those netting bags that comes with a packet of carrots at the greengrocer's. However, it will soon get rather messy and, in the long run, it is best to buy a wire basket specially made for the job.

Scrap baskets made of collapsible wire mesh must be avoided as, with these, there is a danger that small birds may get a foot jammed between two moving pieces of wire. Sharp edges and potential leg-damagers must, in fact, be watched for on all feeding devices. Many small birds get leg injuries, and it may be that ill-made bird feeders are often to blame. One unusual hazard with small scrap baskets is that they may be stolen by crows. All the crow family are enthusiastic collectors, and I well remember a rook once stealing a bar of soap from my camp site. If you find your scrap basket being borrowed in this way, fix the replacement more securely!

Seed hoppers

The only practical way of providing seed is from a hopper. All other methods are very wasteful. (Even the hopper is susceptible to the aggressive methods of jays and great tits, which scatter mixed seed while searching for titbits.) It is important to keep the seed dry and the hopper must have a good roof. The RSPB supply one which fits neatly into the roof of their standard bird table. (See page 105 for more information.) If you have been on autumn collecting expeditions, you will have a stock of your own seeds; if not, any pet shop will supply you with mixed wild bird seed or canary seed. Keep the hopper well filled, and do not risk a supply-failure in bad weather, because the finches will have become dependent on your generosity.

Nuts

Peanuts are a bird's best friend except in the breeding season, and the best way to present them is to have a special wire-netting box, preferably with a solid roof to keep the shelled nuts dry. (The RSPB and other bird furniture suppliers make excellent grille peanut feeders.) You may find yourself buying 3lb of nuts a week, but it will be in a good cause. If you hang whole peanuts, do not use multi-thread cotton or tits may get their legs trapped between the strands.

49

The best plan is to take a thin piece of galvanized wire, about 18in long, and cut it obliquely at one end to make a sharp point on which to skewer the nuts. Bend the top end into a hanging hook, and the bottom end slightly up to prevent the peanuts sliding off. Attach the wire to its anchor point by an elastic band, and the whole thing will twist around as birds perch on it. Tits particularly seem to enjoy twirling round in circles and are very amusing to watch. The peanut skewer can hang from the bird table or from a bough. Do not buy any of the feeders which are made of spiral wire which terminates in a point at the lower end. These are great leg-traps and should be avoided at all costs. (See page 107 for various nut-feeders which can be safely recommended.)

Some Americans recommend clamping a jar of peanut butter to a bird table, and though I have not tried this myself, it should be worth experiment. But don't offer the stuff too freely, for it is a bit too sticky, and may clamp a bird's mandibles together. Mix equal parts of cornmeal with the peanut butter. You can prevent rain from getting in by fixing the jar at a slight downhill angle. For other uses of nuts you might like to try jamming brazils into odd cracks and crannies in trees; nuthatches will appreciate this sort of treasure hunt. Any chestnuts you have collected in the autumn can be boiled and crushed for the tits. Hazel nuts, acorns and beech-mast should be grated or chopped.

Bird-Bell

It was the well-known naturalist H. Mortimer Batten who made the tit-bell famous in the early days of *Children's Hour* on radio, and for many years his wooden design was made available to garden bird enthusiasts. Sadly it is no longer produced, but Robert Gillmor and I have persuaded the Dartmouth Pottery to make a glazed version which does the job quite well (see pages 51 and 107). In essence it is a very simple device, making it possible to use up kitchen scraps in a way that allows only the most agile birds to get them, with a certain amount of difficulty. Thus the 'greedy' starlings and sparrows are held at arm's length. The pottery bell is turned upside down and placed in a mug or bowl and thus held firmly. It is primed with scraps and seeds, has a perch twig set in it, and is then filled with hot fat (not the sort which stays liquid at room temperature, though). When the mixture has set, you hang the bell up for tits, nuthatches and woodpeckers to explore. One of the advantages of the bird-bell is that it lasts a long time between replenishments, so it keeps your birds happy if you have to go away. Even the ground feeders get some benefit, when small pieces get dislodged and fall down. If you do not wish to buy the bird-bell you can make a perfectly good substitute from a half-coconut, the original and cheapest version!

Another useful hanging device is the suet stick. For this, bore 1in holes through a short length of birch log, stuff the holes with raw beef or kidney suet and hang it up. Woodpeckers are very fond of this gadget, but avoid fancy perches, or the starlings will take over (see drawing, page 52).

Ground feeding stations

Many birds are reluctant to come to the bird table. Blackbirds and thrushes, dunnock and even moorhens will all prefer to feed on the ground. The best plan is to put down a special tray for them, so that it can be taken in at night. Otherwise you will be encouraging rats. Do not put the tray too near a possible cat hiding-place, but see that it is within about 6ft or so of cover. Just outside my window, as I write, there are three dunnocks, a pair of yellowhammers, a chaffinch and a greenfinch all feeding happily on the ground below the bird table. Great tits get into the bird table seed-hopper and scatter the seeds as they search for bits of walnut, so that there are always easy pickings on the ground below. Many birds will hunt for crumbs under a bird table, and you may prefer to provide these groundfeeders with a nut-hopper of their own. If you are plagued with sparrows, a coarse wheat-hopper placed well away from your more expensive seed devices may keep them occupied.

Not all of the seeds which fall to the ground will be found and eaten by birds. Some may lie there and, in due course, germinate. And your bird table may sprout in due course from a truly exotic garden of unexpected plants.

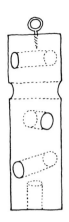

David McClintock, the distinguished botanist, carried out some fascinating experiments in which, instead of offering commercial bird food to the birds, he planted it. He was puzzled by the strange names which were given by the seedsmen, and found, after much research, that seeds called 'Blue Maw' and 'Dari', which are not found in botanical books, revealed themselves as opium poppy *Papaver somniferum* and the annual tropical cereal *Sorghum bicolor* when they were encouraged to grow and reveal themselves as plants.

For the enthusiast, I reproduce the table which crowned his efforts, first published in the periodical *New Scientist*.

Aniseed	*Pimpinella anisum*
Blue maw	*Papaver somniferum*
Buckwheat	*Fagopyrum esculentum*
Mazagan canary	*Phalaris canariensis*
Chicory	*Cichorium intybus*
Dari	*Sorghum bicolor*
Gold of pleasure	*Camelina sativa*
Hemp	*Cannabis sativa*
White kardi	*Carthamnus tinctorius*
White lettuce	*Lactuca sativa*
Best Dutch linseed	*Linum usitassimum*
Chinese millet	*Setaria italica*
Japanese millet	*Echinochloa utilis*
Plate yellow millet	*Panicum miliaceum*
White millet	*Panicum miliaceum*
Niger	*Guizotia abyssinica*
Panicum millet	*Setaria italica*
Black rape	*Brassica campestris*
German rübsen	*Brassica campestris*
Chinese safflower	*Carthamnus tinctorius*
Striped sunflower seed	*Helianthus annuus*
French teazle	*Dipsacus sativus*

Window-sills

Even if you do not have a garden, you can still have a lot of fun providing a specialised bird-feeding station at your window-sill. You might devise a special adaptor for clamping the bird table to a sill, and most of the hanging devices can easily be suspended from a bracket. And even if you have a splendid garden, a window-sill feeding station is still desirable because, as sparrows and starlings are shy of it, you will be able to put out special delicacies for special birds. If possible, use a window-sill that is reasonably sheltered from both hot sun and cold winds. And, whatever feeding arrangements you may have, always remember that a constant supply of water is absolutely essential.

Selection problems

Some people have a most unreasonable hatred of starlings. Personally, I find them beautiful and amusing to watch, although they can, occasionally, rather overwhelm one's facilities by sheer weight of numbers. By almost every post in the winter I get letters from people asking how they can make sure that other birds besides starlings get their fair share of the food. Sparrows, too, can be a nuisance as they tend to dominate other birds.

One way to cheat the starlings is to feed early or late. Starlings are late risers, and as they also flock away to roost early in the afternoon, you can cheat them with early morning and evening feeds for your garden residents. Another trick is to make a feeding cage of wire-mesh netting with an aperture too narrow for starlings to penetrate. If you put 1⅛in welded mesh netting round your bird table, it should keep the starlings out. The only disadvantage is that it also keeps thrushes and blackbirds out.

Starlings and sparrows tend to be shyer than other birds, so if you provide a feeding patch for them well away from your house and bird table, they may patronise it in preference to the 'home' feeding stations. This is where a window-sill comes into its own, providing tits, robins and finches with a reward for their tameness. I have already mentioned that a wheat-hopper may keep your sparrows busy while you feed tasty morsels to your favourites.

But do try to develop a more friendly attitude towards starlings. One of their problems, from a bird-gardener's point of view, is that there are so many of them, and it is odd to realise that only a hundred years or so ago they were quite rare in some parts of the country. One of my correspondents, Mrs Dorothy Coomber of Bridlington in Yorkshire, had a starling which was part of the wild household for fourteen years. Recognisable because of a deformed foot, it soon became tame and was fed regularly. For many years she has brought her fledglings to be fed and, when Mrs Coomber moved to another house a short distance away, the starling followed suit! The bird's favourite food is cheese, and it has to be *Cheshire* cheese; no other is acceptable.

If you can feed at the same time every day, it is far and away the best

Great spotted woodpecker (*Eric Hosking*)

Robin at bird table (*Walter Murray/NHPA*)

Great and blue tits (*Eric Hosking*)

method. Animals have built-in clocks and appreciate regularity. Early morning is best of all, as birds lose weight overnight and need a good start to the day. Obviously, the most important season for feeding is winter, when natural food supplies are scarce, and during a hard spell you may hold the lives of many small birds in your hands. So once again, I must emphasise that once you start feeding you must not stop, until the warm days of spring. It is far better not to put out scraps at all if it is likely that, having started, you may later have to stop. The birds soon become dependent on your daily supplies, and if they are not forthcoming during cold weather when the ground is hard with frost, many of your customers die. It is true that they have feathers which insulate them from the cold, but a body cannot function and keep warm without fuel.

At the beginning of April, gradually reduce the amount of food you put out. The pattern of feeding should be altered. The amounts of heating foods such as suet and hemp should be severely reduced, and less bread should be given as this may fill a nestling bird with low-value bulk. Stale cake is better than peanuts for nestlings, but live insect food is best of all, and this is what the parents supply. At this time of year it is arguably best not to feed at all, since most garden birds alter their feeding habits to take advantage of the abundance of insect food. Put out some mealworms and ant pupae, if you wish, though this is the season when the birds are repaying you for your winter largesse. They will destroy hordes of insect pests far more safely than any chemical pesticide.

If you feed throughout the spring, summer and autumn, use very much smaller quantities. This will keep your birds tame and, when you start increasing their supplies in late autumn, your happy band of pensioners will already know the ropes.

5 Predators and poisons

A bird's life is fraught with natural hazards. After surviving a cold winter, it may get snapped up by a sparrowhawk. If it succeeds in finding a mate and hatching young, there may be a sudden shortage of food and the weaker nestlings may die. The chances of a wild bird living to a ripe old age are so remote as to be almost non-existent. So if we are going to invite birds to join us in our gardens there is an obligation on us to try to reduce the hazards, while recognising the fact that the predator-prey relationship is basically a healthy one, with advantages for both parties.

Ideally, of course, you should completely seal your garden from unwelcome predators, but this is more easily said than done. Sparrowhawks and weasels are all part of the natural scene (weasels are adept at raiding nestboxes), but domestic cats and grey squirrels are less acceptable. Ideally, there is no place for them in the bird garden, but you will never keep them out, short of total war. If you have a cat of your own, you may like to consider keeping it in for a reasonable and regular period each morning and before dusk, in order to give the birds time to feed. I have to admit that I like the company of a cat, and would not care to be without one, but the fact remains that Great Britain is home to many millions of cats, every one of them superfluous to a good bird garden. You must make your own decisions, but one thing is certain. You should not try to *tame* your garden birds if you keep a cat. Feed them and make homes for them by all means, but don't encourage them to become too friendly or there will, inevitably, be a tragic outcome.

If you don't want to go as far as installing a wire fence, the best substitute is a thick and prickly hedge. Hawthorn or holly hedges will both in time become fairly impenetrable, although you will always have to watch for secret passageways and block them with bramble or thorn cuttings. The disadvantage of a clipped hedge is that it will not fruit very freely, though, on the other hand, it provides good nesting sites. Allow some of the plants to mature so that a few trees grow out of the hedge to blossom and fruit. Holly is particularly good, because the dead leaves cover the soil underneath with spiny points which may deter cats, weasels, and such like.

Rats have to be taken seriously. They climb well, even shinning up trees and hedges to search for eggs and young birds, and a good bird garden is also an attractive rat garden. So food should not be left on the ground at night, and windfalls too should be cleared away every evening: they can become part of the winter bird table menu.

The best way to deal with rats is to use a safe poison, or to put plenty of traps under cover in the dark places they like. Place a 5–6ft drainpipe (6in section) in the likely places, and put a killer food bait – 'Raticate' or 'Warfarin' are probably the safest – in the middle of it. Mechanical rat-traps are only moderately successful. Rats are suspicious creatures and if you try traps put one each side of a bait placed in the middle of the pipe-length. Cheese, apple, cake, almost anything will do as bait. Set the traps before dusk and examine them when it is dark. Don't leave them set up all night or you might trap a cat.

Grey squirrels, too, are unwelcome visitors to the bird garden. They may appear charmingly acrobatic as they leap from branch to branch, but they are great egg-eaters. They will even enlarge the hole of a nestbox to lift out the nestlings. You must harden your heart and shoot or trap them. You might want to discourage jays and magpies, for there is no doubt that they will take any small birds' eggs and young they can find. On the other hand, they are handsome birds in their own right.

The greatest bird menace of all is the organo-chlorine insecticide. After years of trial and a growing weight of evidence against them, it is depressing to find that farmers still use dangerous seed-dressings and sprays, and that garden shops still sell harmful and extravagant garden 'aids'. If you have the least feeling for wildlife and, incidentally, if you value your own health, you should refuse to use organo-chlorine pesticides and you should encourage others to do the same. Our environment is becoming increasingly polluted with chemicals whose long-term effects are unknown but highly suspect. Many of the pesticides sold freely in shops are dangerous, not only to the pests they set out to destroy but to useful animals, as well as, ultimately, to ourselves.

Nowadays, unlike the sad days of 1960 and '61, when enormous numbers of

Grey squirrel (*Jeffrey Taylor*)

birds died as a result of ignorant use of toxic chemicals, the situation has improved. The sight of birds falling from the sky or writhing in agony has become quite rare, but the present relatively stable position with regard to birds of prey is not comfortable enough for any complacency. There is not much doubt that many farmers stockpiled dangerous chemicals such as Aldrin and Dieldrin before the ban was introduced; and dangerous sheep-dips and seed-dressings are still being used. Only a few heavily contaminated prey are needed to kill a hawk, falcon or owl. And even if the bird is not killed, its fertility may be affected.

I do not suggest that we stop waging war against garden pests, but it is worth pointing out that sprays do dangerously just that which birds do safely. Finches, tits, tree-creepers and wrens all patrol and police leafy places and control the caterpillar and insect population. Thrushes (and hedgehogs) help with your snails and slugs. Encourage the birds, save yourself money, and give yourself pleasure at the same time. It is true that birds will also eat some of your soft fruit and spoil some of the buds of your fruit trees, but this is a small price to pay for the pleasure they will give and for the knowledge that yours is a poison-free garden. On balance, birds do more good than harm.

In general, herbicidal chemicals which are used to destroy unwanted plants are not directly harmful to birds and other animals or insects. The instructions given on the label should always be carefully followed, however, and it is recommended that they are only used when absolutely necessary. Remember that quite a small patch of rough grass and nettles can bring attractive birds and insects to your garden. If you must use chemical preparations, please:

1 Read the label on the container *and* the manufacturer's instruction leaflets, and ensure that the recommended dosages are used.

2 Take particular care against spillage when mixing chemicals.

3 Never spray in windy weather likely to cause spray drift.

4 When spraying near water-courses, take every precaution to avoid water pollution.

5 Never wash or clean equipment in water-courses.

6 Return, burn, or flatten and bury used containers.

7 Keep spraying equipment in good order.

8 Ensure that partly used containers are tightly closed and clearly labelled, and never transfer chemicals to other containers.

9 Store both full and partly-used containers in a locked store.

In contrast to the herbicides, some insecticides are extremely harmful to wildlife, being either very poisonous or very persistent. The Ministry of Agriculture, Fisheries and Food has said that insecticides containing *Aldrin* and *Dieldrin* are no longer permitted and present information indicates that *DDT*, *BHC* and also arsenic-based compounds should be avoided. Note that these are not, necessarily, the brand names displayed in large type on the label. One must read the small type on the tin or packet to discover whether the preparation is dangerous or not. Any chemical should be used sparingly, with care and according to the directions on the label; ideally it should not be used at all.

Recommended alternatives

These are relatively non-poisonous to birds and mammals, and are not persistent.

1 Derris (or Rotenone), but note that this insect-killer is very toxic to fish, so do not use it if there is any likelihood of it finding its way into a pond or stream.

2 Pyrethrum, another potent insect-killer which is not harmful to warm-blooded creatures.

Pyrethrins are extracted from a white-flowered crop grown in the highlands of Kenya, and are the basis of a number of safe pesticides. As insects do not build up a resistance to pyrethrum it is more efficient in the long run, although it may not have quite the sensational and immediate effect of some of the dangerous organo-chlorine preparations. But use the spray in the evening, to spare the bees. Pyrethrum will control most flying and crawling insect pests such as ants, blackfly, caterpillars, flea beetles, greenfly, sawfly, whitefly and thrips.

3 Malathion, an organo–phosphorus compound, but do not use on certain plants, eg antirrhinum and fuchsia. Trichlophon and Fenitrothion are other organo–phosphates with low toxicity to mammals.

4 Carbaryl, a carbamate compound, but avoid using on apple trees between late pink bud and the end of the first week in June, because it is dangerous to bees and affects the early development of fruit.

5 Tar oil, with or without petroleum oil, on dormant fruit trees.

Pest	Recommended treatment
Aphis (greenfly, blackfly)	When these are exposed, as on many pot plants, aphids can be washed off with a spray of soapy water. Otherwise derris spray, malathion or pyrethrum
Caterpillars (cabbage white)	Derris dust, malathion, pyrethrum, trichlophon
Flies (adult blow and house)	Pyrethrum
Some fruit pests and wasps' nests	Derris
Aphids (on fruit trees)	Petroleum/tar oil (dormant trees) malathion
Blackcurrant gall mite (big bud)	Lime sulphur, sulphur, but do not use either on redcurrants
Capsids (sucking bugs)	Carbaryl, malathion, petroleum/tar oil (dormant trees)
Caterpillars (codlin, tortrix, winter-moth eggs laid on dormant trees)	As above

Red spider mite	As for caterpillars above
Scale insects	As above
Woolly aphid	Malathion

Slug control

Metaldehyde and Mathiocarb are the active ingredients in the majority of pellets, etc at present on the market. Little is known about their toxicity to birds, although methiocarb is suspected of being the more poisonous of the two. Hedgehogs may also be poisoned, either directly by the bait or from eating the dead slugs. Slug bait should therefore be covered with a board, brick or flower pot to prevent birds and other mammals feeding on it. It should also be used away from children and pets. Slugs are attracted to substances with a high sugar content (including beer). They can be collected if the liquid is put in a smooth-sided container out of which they cannot climb. If you must use slug-bait, use Fertosan.

Bullfinch deterrent on buds

Anthraquinone, which is used in certain trade preparations, is a relatively non-poisonous substance. However, it cannot be guaranteed to protect buds under all conditions.

Fungicides

Caution: those based on mercury, including calomel (mercurious chloride) and organo-mercury compounds used on fruit trees, cannot be recommended because of their persistence. Certain of them could poison wildlife.

Finally, to save yourself needless expense and to develop a healthy poison-free garden, get a copy of a most excellent and invaluable booklet *Pest control without Poisons*, by Lawrence D. Hills, published by the Henry Doubleday Research Association, Bocking, Braintree, Essex.

And please don't ask me to define what is and what is not a pest, because I have the uncomfortable feeling that you and I might be prime candidates. Live and let live.

6 Species

There are no identification notes in the following list, which is arranged in the Wetmore order of classification, as listed in the BTO 'Species list of British and Irish Birds' (available from BTO, address on page 112).

One of the best reference books for bird identification is *A Field Guide to the Birds of Britain and Europe*, by Peterson, Mountfort and Hollom, published by Collins. For identification notes plus detailed information on habitat, distribution, behaviour, food and breeding (in the wild) the most useful single volume is *The Popular Handbook of British Birds*, by P. A. D. Hollom, published by H. F. and G. Witherby. Further information on nestboxes can be found in the pamphlet *Nestboxes*, published by the BTO.

Additions and corrections to the food preference and nestbox sections in the following notes will be welcomed.

GREAT CRESTED GREBE. *Podiceps cristatus*. Breeds regularly in most English counties except Devon and Cornwall. Scarcer in Scotland and Wales. Lakes, reservoirs, gravel pits and large ponds with reedy cover. Dives for fish, insects, tadpoles, etc.

Naturally nests among reeds or vegetation close to edge. Will accept a man-made raft (see page 28).

FULMAR. *Fulmarus glacialis*. Summer visitor, breeding on coastal cliffs more or less round the whole of the British Isles. Otherwise at sea in the North Atlantic. Feeds on molluscs, fish, etc. Takes fish-offal thrown overboard from fishing vessels. Nests on cliff slopes and ledges. Has taken to excavated ledges provided in crumbly Norfolk cliffs by Gresham's School Natural History Society.

Read: *The Fulmar* by James Fisher, Collins, 1952.

GREY HERON. *Ardea cinerea.* May come to bird table for kitchen scraps, will come to garden pond for goldfish, etc.

Read: *The Heron* by Frank A. Lowe, Collins, 1954.

MALLARD (Wild Duck). *Anas platyrhynchos.* Resident and generally distributed. Fresh water, sea coast and estuary.

Feeds on seeds, buds, leaves of land and water plants, insects and other small water animals. Will come to suitable feeding stations in shallow water for corn or to water's edge for scraps, although this will depend on the degree of tameness achieved. (Many wild mallard join semi-domesticated duck collections.)

Nests in thick undergrowth not far from water. Sometimes in pollard willows, tree holes, second-hand crow-type nests, etc. Grass, leaves, rushes, feathers, down. Lays about a dozen eggs, greyish-green or greenish-buff, occasionally clear pale blue, February onwards. Incubation, 4 weeks; fledging, $7\frac{1}{2}$ weeks. 1 or 2 broods.

Nestbox: Try providing an apple box or large, open cat basket in typical nest site. Where mallards have become very tame (in village ponds and the like) try erecting an open-ended barrel on an island. But the most picturesque, as well as the most efficient box, is the Dutch nesting-basket, an open-weave affair with something of the shape of those old-fashioned water pitchers (available from Sutton Parva Nurseries, page 107). The diameter of the entrance hole should be about 6in, and this measurement is important. Placed on stakes just above the water, the basket should be tilted upwards until it is at an angle of about 20 to 30 degrees from the horizontal. This forces the duck to lay at the far end, as far from a crow's beak as possible. But if the water level fluctuates, the basket is safer on a raft.

Read: *Wildfowl in Great Britain*, edited by G. Atkinson-Willes, Nature Conservancy Monograph No 3, HMSO, 1965; *Wildfowl Management*, Eley Game Advisory Station, Fordingbridge, Hampshire, 1969.

GADWALL. *Anas strepera.* Will on occasion nest on rafts.

TUFTED DUCK. *Aythya fuligula.* Will occasionally nest on rafts.

SHELDUCK. *Tadorna tadorna.* May be persuaded to nest in a fruit box in an artificial hollow in vegetation, for instance wild rose or bramble bushes surrounded by long grass or bracken.

GREYLAG GOOSE. *Anser anser.* Has regularly nested on rafts in suitable locations.

CANADA GOOSE. *Branta canadensis.* Resident and widely distributed. An introduced species. Grassland and marshes near lakes, meres.

Grazes in flocks on grassland. Also takes water plants. Will come to hand-feed on corn or bread when tame.

Nests on islands and marshes, sheltered by undergrowth or bush. Nest-hollow lined with grasses, leaves, reeds, down and feathers. 5 or 6 white eggs.

Late March/April. Incubation, 4 weeks; fledging, 6 weeks. 1 brood.

Nestbox: Box or platform raised on posts above water-level or on raft. Make an artificial island, plant clumps of iris, reeds, sedge, etc, to provide artificial nest site. *Warning!* Canada geese (gander especially) can be very aggressive in the breeding season, and have been known to attack human beings, even wounding children.

MUTE SWAN. *Cygnus olor.* Generally distributed. Open water, ponds, parks, sheltered sea coasts and lochs.

Dips head and neck, or 'up-ends' to graze on underwater vegetation; also takes roots and buds of aquatic plants, small frogs, tadpoles, fish. Will come to hand or feeding station for scraps.

Nests almost anywhere near water, in a large heap of vegetation. 5–7 eggs, almost white, tinged with greyish or bluish green. April/May. Incubation, about 35 days; fledging, about 4½ months. 1 brood. *Warning!* Aggressive at nest.

Nestbox: Artificial island or raft, primed with a pile of vegetation.

Read: *The Royal Birds*, Lillian Grace Paca, St Martin's Press, New York, 1963; *The Swans*, Sir Peter Scott and The Wildfowl Trust, 1972.

SPARROWHAWK. *Accipiter nisus.* May come to bird table to carry off small birds. Be philosophic about this; sparrowhawks have to make a living too!

MERLIN. *Falco columbarius.* Might be seen chasing small birds in feeding area, if you're lucky.

KESTREL. *Falco tinnunculus.* Resident, generally distributed, except in winter in far north. At present decreasing in numbers. Moors, coast, farmland and open woodland.

Perches on trees, posts, wires or buildings, watching out for its prey. Hunts in the open, checking frequently to hover in characteristic attitude, watching for beetles or small mammals. Untypically, has been known to come to a bird table in hard weather for broken dog-biscuit.

Makes no nest, but lays eggs in a scrape on cliff ledge or in second-hand crow or magpie nest. Sometimes in tree hollow or ledge on building or ruin. About 5 eggs, the white ground colour often hidden by red-brown splotchings. Mid-April onwards. Incubation 28 days; fledging, 28 days. 1 brood.

Nestbox: Open-fronted type, 25in by 15in by 15in high, with roof overhanging a couple of inches. One of the long sides is partly open, having only a 5in high board along the bottom part, fitted with a broom-pole size lip to enable the bird to perch easily before entering. Prime the box with some peat mould. Fix very firmly on 18–30ft pole, or high on side of house, where some shelter is available from midday sun.

Swiss-erected boxes were positioned near farm buildings, and in one year no fewer than 26 out of 36 were occupied in an area of about 5,000 acres. With the continuing loss of hedgerow hollow-tree sites it is much to be hoped that these boxes will become more popular with farmers. But it makes a conspicuous nest

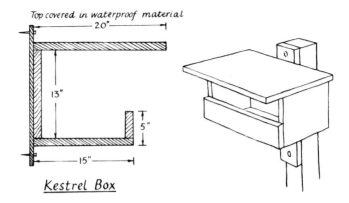

Top covered in waterproof material

13"

20"

5"

15"

Kestrel Box

site, and unfortunately young kestrels have a ready, though illegal, market, so be very careful that they are well protected. Farm buildings, private parkland, nature reserves and sewage farms are ideal sites. Not only kestrels, but little owl, jackdaw, collared dove, stock dove or blackbird may use these boxes.

PHEASANT. *Phasianus colchicus*. Resident and generally distributed except in Ireland. Much-preserved as a game bird. Woodland edge, cultivated land, parkland, large secluded gardens and shrubberies, damp, rushy and sedgy fields.

Forages on ground for varied selection of animal and vegetable food. Fruit, seeds, grain, insects, worms, slugs. Will come to secluded garden ground station for corn.

Nests under cover of ferns, brambles, etc, in woods, copses, hedgerows and reed-beds, making a hollow in the ground and lining it with a few stems of grass and dead leaves. 8–15 olive-brown eggs. Early April onwards. Incubation, 22–27 days; fledging, 12–14 days. 1 brood.

MOORHEN. (Waterhen). *Gallinula chloropus*. Resident and widely distributed. Fresh-water ponds, slow streams, marshes and water-meadows.

Forages on grassland and waterside vegetation. Food is mostly vegetable, but includes a fair proportion of animals, such as worms, slugs, and snails. Will soon get used to coming to scraps on the ground; flies less readily up on to the bird table. Watch out for rats.

Nests among waterside plants or trees, building an open structure of reeds, flags, sedge, etc. 5–11 eggs, whitish-grey to buff or greenish with suffused red-brown spots. End of March onwards. Incubation 19–22 days; fledging period: in nest 2 or 3 days if undisturbed, then another 3–5 weeks with family. Generally 2 broods.

Read: *A Waterhen's Worlds*, by H. Eliot Howard, Cambridge University Press, 1940.

Wood pigeon drinking (*E. A. Janes/NHPA*)

COOT. *Fulica atra*. Has regularly nested on rafts.

TURNSTONE. *Arenaria interpres*. Winter visitor to rocky or pebbly coasts, although many non-breeders stay for the summer.

Roots about in small parties over rocks or shore, searching for small seashore animals in weed and tide-line debris. Comes eagerly to regular beach feeding station for bread, cake, peanuts and scraps in South Devon, and I suggest others should try the experiment. (Winwood Reade tells me that turnstones also come to feed outside the army camp kitchen on the remote island of St Kilda.)

Breeds from Arctic Circle to points north.

HERRING GULL. *Larus argentatus*. Resident, generally distributed along coasts, estuaries, waters and fields often far inland.

Opportunist feeder, eating almost anything, but mostly animal food. Will come to bird table or ground station for almost anything, but is shy and not particularly welcomed by other birds.

Nests in colonies on cliff ledges, grassy coastal slopes, sand dunes and shingle. Large nest of grass or sea-weed. About 3 eggs, olive to umber, sometimes pale blue or green, splotched with deep blackish-brown. End April to early June. Incubation, 26 days; fledging, 6 weeks. 1 brood. Of recent years it has taken to nesting on roofs and chimney pot areas where scraps are freely available. Not to be encouraged, though, as it can be aggressive in defence of its young.

Read: *The Herring Gull's World*, Niko Tinbergen, Collins, 1953.

BLACK-HEADED GULL. *Larus ridibundus*. Resident and widely distributed. Coastal and inland species frequenting lakes, sewage-farms, harbours and farmland.

Feeds around low-lying shores and estuaries, freely inland to farms, lakes and rivers. Food very varied, animal and vegetable. Will come fairly freely to bird feeding stations in open situations.

Nests in colonies among sandhills, sandbanks, lake islands and shingle. Rough nest of vegetable matter. About 3 eggs, light buffish-stone to deep umber brown, splotched dark blackish-brown. Mid-April onwards. Incubation, 22–24 days; fledging, 6 weeks. 1 brood.

KITTIWAKE. *Rissa tridactyla*. Nests in colonies on precipitous sea-cliff ledges. Has enjoyed man's hospitality by colonising cliff-ledge-like warehouse window-ledges.

COMMON TERN. *Sterna hirundo*. Has been known to take bread in company with gulls feeding in the wake of a ferry (Torpoint, Devonport). Will nest on rafts (see page 28).

STOCK DOVE. *Columba oenas*. Resident and well distributed, except in northern Scotland. Open parkland, wooded country, cliffs and sand dunes.

Feeds over fields and open ground, taking vegetable leaves, beans, peas and grain.

Nests in holes in old trees, rocks, rabbit-burrows, buildings. Insubstantial structure of few twigs, bits of grass, or nothing at all. 2 creamy-white eggs.

End March till July. Incubation, 16–18 days; fledging, 28 days. 2, sometimes - even 3, broods.

Nestbox: Enclosed. 8in diameter entrance hole, 15in interior depth, 15in by 25in floor. Or alternatively, box similar to that for kestrel, but mounted on tree.

ROCK PIGEON. *Columba livia.* Resident, but decreasing in numbers and hopelessly inter-bred with its own descendant, the domestic pigeon. The only pure rock doves that remain are probably to be found on the north and west coasts of Scotland and Ireland. Rocky sea-cliffs and coastal fields.

Forages on coastal pastureland for grain, peas, beans, potatoes, seeds, etc.

Nests in sea-caves or among rocks in wilder parts of coast. Few bits of heather or roots in a hole or cave-ledge or crevice. 2 white eggs, April onwards. Incubation, 17–19 days; fledging, 4 or 5 weeks. 2 or 3 broods.

Rock doves were domesticated hundreds of years ago in Scotland. Artificial nesting ledges were provided for them in convenient sea-caves, and the resulting squabs farmed for food. The flourishing domestic forms of the rock dove (feral pigeons) have confused the wild status of the bird in no uncertain fashion. The feral pigeon breeds freely in cities and places where it can take advantage of man's soft heart and kitchen scraps.

WOOD PIGEON (Ring Dove). *Columba palumbus.* Resident and generally distributed except in extreme north of Scotland. Open country of all kinds, provided there are some trees.

Feeds mainly on ground, but in spring will graze over foliage, buds and flowers in trees. Main food vegetable, cereals, roots, beans, peas and seeds. Will come to garden feeding station for ground food, bread, vegetable scraps, seeds, and may even visit the bird table. Partial to beans and peas.

Nests in tall hedgerows, almost any kind of tree, second-hand crow nests and squirrel dreys. Sometimes on ground or on building ledges in towns, where it has overcome shyness. Few twigs (you can often see the outline of the eggs if you stand under the flimsy nest). Normally 2 white eggs. April to September. Incubation, 17 days; fledging, about 3 weeks. 3 broods usually.

Read: *The Wood Pigeon*, R. K. Murton, Collins, 1965.

COLLARED DOVE. *Streptopelia decaocto.* Resident and widely distributed. Vicinity of farm-buildings, park-like places and gardens in towns and villages.

Finds its food in close relationship with man, sharing grain with chickens, raiding corn and stackyards. In parks and gardens will also take berries and young foliage. Comes freely to bird table and ground feeding station for seeds, peas, grain and scraps.

Nests in trees, preferably conifers, on a flimsy platform of sticks, grasses and roots. 2 white eggs. March to October. Several broods.

As recently as 1954 this species did not figure on the British List, yet it is now found throughout the country, the result of a remarkable cross-Europe invasion originating from India.

BARN OWL. *Tyto alba*. Resident, generally distributed, but not abundant. Vicinity of farms, old buildings, church towers, etc. Parkland with old timber. Hunts over fields and open country for small rodents and even small birds.

Nests in ruins or unoccupied buildings, hollow trees and cliff crevices. No material used, the eggs are often surrounded by a pile of castings. 4–7 white eggs. April to July. Incubation, 32–34 days; fledging, about 10 weeks. Frequently 2 broods.

Nestbox: Open tray 36in long, 15in wide and 12in deep. Divide interior into two equal areas with a crosswise partition 7in or 8in deep. A two-compartment apple box serves the purpose, with the top 6in of the middle partition knocked out. The tray should be placed just inside and below a large entrance hole to a suitable building, loft or large recess well above the ground. The owls will nest in the section of the tray further from the hole. The other section is for the adults to leave prey items. It may be preferable to site the tray away from the entrance hole, if there is an owl-attractive dark and quiet place. Cover the floor of the tray with a thin scattering of dry peat or sawdust.

Read: *Owls*, John Sparks and Tony Soper, David & Charles, 1971.

LITTLE OWL. *Athene noctua*. An introduced species, now resident in the southern half of England. Open farmland.

Hunts mainly at dusk and early morning for small mammals, insects and a few birds.

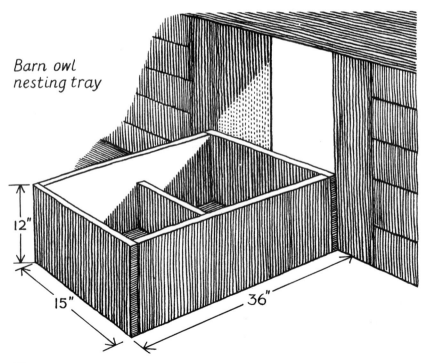

Barn owl
nesting tray

12"

15"

36"

Nests in trees, farm-building holes and rabbit burrows. 3–5 white eggs. April, May. Incubation, 28–29 days; fledging, about 26 days. Usually 1 brood.

Nestbox: Enclosed type, at least 4in diameter hole, inside depth 12in, floor 57sq in. Also open type similar to kestrel box. Newest design, successfully pioneered in Southern Germany, is based on a 'hollow branch'. Take two round, equal-sized, wooden discs of softwood, approx 2in thick and not less than 6in diameter. Bore a 2¾in entrance hole in one disc. Form a drum by nailing wooden slats 39 × 1 × ½in on to the discs which should be 31½in apart. Secure the drum with wire and wrap it with a layer of roofing felt. Camouflage with a layer of rush mat or loose bark and fasten with wire. Mount on a thick horizontal branch some 10–16ft high, the drum sloping slightly to the rear. Don't expose the entrance to the prevailing wind. Prime with garden peat. It seems important that the interior is not less than 31½in long and the closed end must be light-proof.

TAWNY OWL. *Strix aluco*. Resident and generally distributed in Great Britain, but never recorded wild in Ireland. Woodland, farmland, parks and well-timbered gardens.

Hunts at dusk for small mammals, birds and insects, even frogs and newts. May take scraps – and small birds – from bird table.

Nests in tree holes, second-hand crow, hawk and heron nests, squirrel dreys. Sometimes in barns and rock ledges. 2–4 white eggs. Late March, early April.

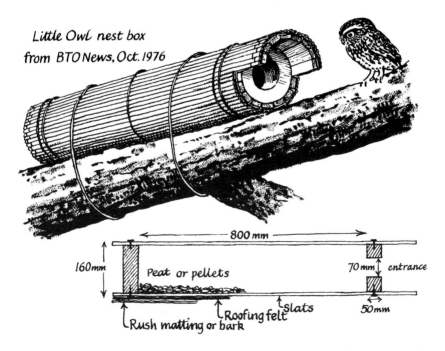

Little Owl nest box from BTO News, Oct. 1976

800 mm

160mm — Peat or pellets — 70 mm entrance

Rush matting or bark — Roofing felt — Slats — 50mm

Incubation, 28–30 days; fledging, about 4 weeks. 1 brood.

Nestbox: Enclosed type, 8in diameter hole at top, inside depth 30in, floor 8 × 8in. Will also use a 9gal cider barrel if a hole is opened in it and the barrel put in a tree crotch about 12ft high, although the height is probably not critical.

Chimney type: See drawing. Four wooden planks at least 30in long and 8in wide butted onto each other, using 2 or 2½in oval nails, to make a square-sectioned chimney. A 9 × 9in base which must be perforated by at least half a dozen drainage holes, is nailed to one end to form the floor. A thin sheet of ferrous metal is to be preferred to either perforated zinc or a wooden floor. A layer of dry peat or sawdust should be added to the completed base to counteract the fouling that will occur in the fledging period. Chimney boxes of this size are too deep for a hand to reach the bottom, either for examining or ringing the nestlings or for cleaning out. It is practical to make an observation door on one side of the box, 8in by 6in, which is hinged to the back of the box and fastened at the front by a hook and eye catch. Fit the box under a lateral tree-bough at an angle of about 30 degrees from the vertical. If attaching to main trunk, contrive an angle of about 45 degrees to simulate 'broken branch'. Secure to the tree by wire bands at both the top and the bottom, but remember these will rust through or become embedded in bark so watch your maintenance.

Read: *Owls*, John Sparks and Tony Soper, David & Charles, 1971.

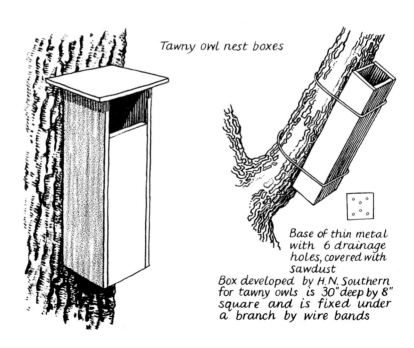

Tawny owl nest boxes

Base of thin metal with 6 drainage holes, covered with sawdust

Box developed by H.N. Southern for tawny owls is 30"deep by 8" square and is fixed under a branch by wire bands

LONG-EARED OWL. *Asio otus*. Has been known to use duck-type nest-baskets (see Mallard) in Holland.

SWIFT. *Apus apus*. Summer resident, generally distributed except in north-west Scotland, arriving late April, early May, leaving early August. Habitat exclusively aerial. Very rarely seen at rest except on the nest.

Feeds on the wing, taking only insects, anywhere from ground level to 1,000ft.

Nests in colonies, under eaves, in crevices and in holes. Bits of straw, grass, feathers, seed fluff, collected on the wing and stuck together with saliva to form a cup. 2 or 3 white eggs. Late May, early June. Incubation, 18–19 days; fledging, about 6 weeks. 1 brood.

Nestbox: Using a plank 65 × 8 × ¾in, make a box 19½ × 8 × 5½in with an entrance-hole 5 × 3in cut in the *floor* of the box (not the end, as swifts prefer to enter vertically from below). Make box longer than 19½in if convenient, but not shorter, as they like to site nest at least 12in from entrance hole. Prime nest site with a ring of twisted straw. Cut an inspection door 6 × 8in at rear roof to aid cleaning. Site it under the eaves at least 12ft above ground, up to 100ft if necessary. Block entrance-hole till swifts arrive, in order to discourage earlier-nesting sparrows and starlings. Or open out a narrow slit in eaves to allow entrance to roof.

Read: *Swifts in a Tower*, David Lack, Methuen, 1956.

KINGFISHER. *Alcedo atthis*. Resident and generally distributed, but scarce and decreasing. Streams, rivers, canals, lakes.

Perches or hovers above water, fish-watching. Plunges to capture small fish, insects, larvae and amphibians. In winter, visits coast for shrimps, prawns, small rock-pool fish, etc. May come to garden ponds for minnows or stickle-backs.

Nests in tunnels in banks of streams or sand-pits. 6–7 white eggs. Late April to August. Incubation, 19–21 days; fledging, 23–27 days. 2 broods.

Nestbox: Will excavate nest-tunnel in artificial bank by suitable stream. See directions in The Wildfowl Trust's bulletin no 73 (September 75).

HOOPOE. *Upupa epops*. Passage-migrant, regular in small numbers in spring, less frequent in autumn, on south, south-east and south-west coasts, and on east coast as far north as Norfolk. Elsewhere rare in Great Britain. Open woodland, orchards, parkland.

Feeds mainly on ground, often close to human habitation, probing on lawns for insect larvae, etc. Does not often come to bird station, but might do so if mealworms/caterpillars/ant pupae were made available in dish. Not shy.

Normally breeds in Eurasia, but occasionally a hoopoe will nest in one of the southern coastal counties, choosing tree holes, crevices and holes in rough stone walls and ruins. 5–8 eggs, whitish-grey or yellowish-olive. May/June. Incubation, 18 days; fledging, 20–27 days. 2 broods.

Nestbox: Uses them in Europe and, presumably, may do so here.

GREEN WOODPECKER. *Picus viridis*. Resident, but local in England and Wales, rare in Scotland, none in Ireland. Deciduous woods, park and farmland.

Searches for insect larvae over tree trunks and branches, probing with long mobile tongue; also feeds freely on ground, especially where there are ant's nests. In times of hard frost, when ant hills are frozen solid, it may damage beehives by boring holes to reach the insects within. May also attack nestboxes. Will visit bird table for mealworms, bird pudding, etc.

Nests in tree trunks, boring a hole horizontally 2–3in, then descending to make a nest compartment over 1ft deep and about 6in wide at its broadest. A few chips at the bottom form the nest. Sometimes, old holes are used again. 5–7 translucent eggs. End April to May. Incubation, 18–19 days; fledging, 18–21 days. 1 brood.

Nestbox: Enclosed type, with 2½in entrance hole 15in interior depth, 5 × 5in floor. Ideal for starlings!

Read: *My Year with the Woodpeckers*, Heinz Sielmann, Barrie & Rockliff, 1959.

GREAT SPOTTED WOODPECKER. *Dendrocopus major*. Resident, widely distributed in England, central and southern Scotland, none in Ireland. Wooded country – coniferous in north, deciduous in south – hedgerows, orchards and large gardens.

Hunts over trees for insect larvae, spiders, seeds and nuts, even wedging a nut into a tree crack to deal with it. Will come to bird table for suet especially; also oats, nuts, boiled fat bacon, hanging fat, or nuts. As adept as tits at feeding upside down.

Nests in tree holes 10ft and higher from ground. Few wood chips form nest. 4–7 white eggs. May to June. Incubation, 16 days; fledging, 18–21 days. 1 brood.

Nestbox: Enclosed type, entrance hole 2in, interior depth 12in, floor 5 × 5in. Also ideal for starlings.

LESSER SPOTTED WOODPECKER. *Dendrocopus minor*. Resident in southern England and Midlands, becoming local and rarer further north. Widely distributed but scattered in Wales. Not in Scotland or Ireland. Same type of country as greater spotted.

Elusive bird, searching upper parts of trees for insect larvae. Will come somewhat nervously and rarely to bird table for fats, nuts and fruit.

Bores nest-hole in decayed soft wood of branch or tree trunk. A few chips make nest. 4–6 translucent eggs, early May to mid-June. Incubation, 14 days; fledging, 21 days. 1 brood.

WRYNECK. *Jynx torquilla*. Summer resident. Decreasing and scarce, possibly as few as one hundred breeding pairs, mostly in East Anglia. Open parkland, heaths, hedgerows, sometimes orchards, gardens.

Picks up insects from tree surface, clinging to trunk like woodpecker. Sometimes on ground, picking up ants, insect larvae. Feeds occasionally at bird tables.

Great spotted woodpecker

Lesser spotted woodpecker

Nests in natural or improved tree or bank holes. No nesting material. 7–10 white eggs. End May till July. Incubation, 12 days; fledging, 19–21 days. Usually 1 brood.

Nestbox: Enclosed, with 1⅜in by 1¼in diameter entrance, 6in interior depth, 5 × 5in floor.

SKYLARK. *Alauda arvensis.* Has been known to feed regularly on bread-and-cheese scraps from a garden of waste ground at the edge of Liverpool. In hard weather may come to seeds at a ground feeding-station.

SWALLOW. *Hirundo rustica.* Summer resident. Generally distributed. Open farmland, meadows, ponds. Spends much time in flight, especially over water, hunting insects from ground level to 500ft. Unlike swift, settles freely on buildings and wires. Seldom on ground, except when collecting mud for nest.

Nests on rafters and joists, building open mud and straw cup, lined with grasses and feathers. 4–5 eggs, white spotted with red-brown. Mid-May till October. Incubation, 15 days; fledging, 3 weeks. Usually 2 broods.

Nestbox: Improvise a simple saucer-shape, or fix a half-coconut or 4in by 4in shallow wooden tray to joist or rafter, even as low as 6ft. Will also use specially adapted house-martin nest placed singly *inside* the building.

HOUSE MARTIN. *Delichon urbica.* Summer resident, generally distributed. Habitat as swallow, but more often near human habitation. Hunts insects on the wing, especially over water. Also on the ground.

Originally a cliff-nester, has progressed to buildings. Nests in colonies on outside walls, under eaves. Cup shape made of mud and lined with straw and feathers. 4–5 white eggs. Late May to October. Incubation 14–15 days; fledging, 19–21 days. Usually 2 broods.

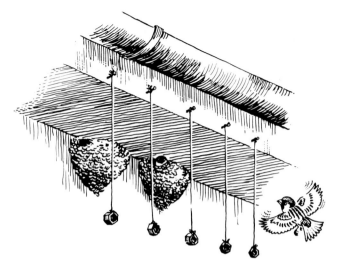

Nestbox: Special artificial nest obtainable from Nerine Nurseries (page 105). Fix under eaves or high window-sill. For best results an existing house-martin colony should be close at hand. One nest may suffice, but the more the merrier. Put them in groups outside, under the horizontal or sloping eaves of houses, barns, etc. The artificial cups are held in position by cup-hooks so that it is possible to slide the nests freely in and out to inspect the contents.

The entrance-hole for house-martin nest cups should be no more than 1in deep, in order to exclude house sparrows. Although the hole is generally proof, there have been cases where the hole has been enlarged and sparrows have gained access. There is a method which has been successful in stopping this, based on the fact that martins are able to approach a nest at a much steeper angle than sparrows. The drawing above illustrates the technique. The hanging cords should not be more than 12in long and should be fixed to hang 6in away from the entrance hole. An interval of $2\frac{1}{2}$in between the cords is effective. In the illustration $\frac{7}{8}$in steel nuts were used as weights. It has been found that by having all the cords the same length they are less likely to get tangled when swaying in a high wind.

It is one of the characteristics of the artificial nests that they frequently encourage house-martins to adopt and make their own nests on a house not previously 'tenanted', but isolated nests away from a colony seem particularly susceptible to attack by sparrows.

SAND MARTIN. *Riparia riparia*. Summer resident, widely distributed. Open country with water.

Feeds mainly over water, taking insects on the wing. Perches on wires and low branches, and will occasionally pick insects from the ground while on the wing.

Nests in colonies, making a long hole with a nest chamber at the end, in sand

and gravel pits, railway cuttings, river banks and sea cliffs. Few straws and feathers from nest. 4–5 white eggs. Mid-May onwards. Incubation, 14 days; fledging, 19 days. 2 broods.

Nestbox: Try boring a few enticing 2in diameter holes in likely sandbanks, steep road cuttings and walls, especially over water (or a length of drainpipe?).

ROOK. *Corvus frugilegus*. Resident and generally distributed. Agricultural areas with trees for nesting.

Feeds openly on ground in small parties or flocks (a lone rook is usually a crow!). Cereals, potatoes, roots, fruit, nuts, berries, insects, worms. Will also feed on carrion (dead lambs, etc), and kill small birds in hard weather. Comes freely to ground station for almost anything.

Nests in tree-top colonies normally. Mass of sticks solidified with earth, lined with grasses and straw. 3–5 light blue-green to green and grey-green eggs. Late March onwards. Incubation, 16–18 days; fledging, 29–30 days. 1 brood.

Read: *The Life of the Rook*, G. K. Yeates, Allan, 1934; *Crows of the World*, Derek Goodwin, British Museum (Natural History) 1976.

JACKDAW. *Corvus monedula*. Resident and common except in north-west Scotland. Farm and parkland, cliffs, old buildings.

Jaunty bird, feeding in parties or flocks on animal and vegetable matter. Will take young birds and eggs if it gets the chance. Comes freely to bird table or ground station for scraps, cereals, potato, fruit, berries and nuts. Fond of macaroni-cheese.

Nests in colonies in trees, buildings, rocks or rabbit burrows, holes, cracks or crevices; almost any hole will do – often in bottom of rook or heron's nest. Nest of twigs, sometimes very bulky, sometimes not. Lining of grass, wool, hair, etc. Usually 4–6 eggs. Pale greenish-blue, spotted brownish-black. Mid-April. Incubation, 17–18 days; fledging, 17–18 days. 1 brood.

Nestbox: Enclosed type, with not less than 6in entrance hole, 17in interior depth, at least 7½ × 7½in floor. Or open type as for kestrel.

Read: *King Solomon's Ring*, Konrad Lorenz, Methuen, 1952; and as rook, above.

MAGPIE. *Pica pica*. Resident and generally distributed in England and Wales, scarce in parts of Scotland. Farmland and open country with hedges and trees.

Frequently in pairs or small parties foraging on ground and in hedgerows for insects, small mammals and birds. Cereals, fruit, nuts, peas and berries. Will come to bird table or ground station for large scraps, which it takes away. Fond of the milk bottle. Not to be too warmly welcomed because of its predatory habits in the breeding season.

Nests in tall trees, thorny bush or neglected hedgerow. Bulky, domed structure of sticks, with an inner lining of earth and roots. 5–8 eggs, greenish-blue to yellowish and greyish-green, spotted and mottled brown and ash. April onwards. Incubation, 17–18 days; fledging, about 22–27 days. 1 brood.

Read: as jackdaw, above.

Jay (*Eric Hosking*)

JAY. *Garrulus glandarius*. Resident and generally distributed. Woodland, never far from trees.

Hops about branches and on ground. Mostly vegetable food, peas, potatoes, corn, beechmast, nuts, fruit and berries. Animal food includes eggs and small birds, mice, slugs, snails, worms and insects. Eats large numbers of acorns and, like other crows, has the habit of burying acorns and other surplus food in secret places in trees and underground. Shy bird, except in some well-timbered suburban areas where it becomes very tame and will come to the bird table or ground station for almost any food. Has learnt to shake spiral peanut-holders to dislodge nuts in order to pick them up from the ground.

Nests fairly low in undergrowth or tree-fork. Sticks and twigs and a little earth, lined with roots and perhaps hair. 5 or 6 sage-green or olive-buff eggs, mottled with darker olive spots. Early May. Incubation, 16–17 days; fledging, 20 days. 1 brood.

Read: as rook, above.

CHOUGH. *Pyrrhocorax pyrrhocorax*. Resident but hard pressed, only some thousand birds left in the British Isles, confined to Scotland, Wales and Ireland. (The Celtic crow, sadly none left in Cornwall now). Nests in crevices or holes in cliffs and sea-caves. Has been known to use artificial covered nest-sites in ruins and such places as Martello Towers.

Great Tit

Blue Tit

Coal Tit

Long-tailed Tit

Marsh Tit

Willow Tit

Read: as rook on page 77.

GREAT TIT. *Parus major*. Resident and generally distributed, scarcer in northern Scotland. Woodland, hedges, gardens.

Forages in trees and hedgerows for insects, spiders, worms. Fruit, peas, nuts and seeds. Does some damage to buds in spring, but it was once estimated that one pair of great tits will destroy 7,000 to 8,000 insects, mainly caterpillars, in about three weeks. Fierce bird that will attack and eat a bee. Comes freely to bird table, to hoppers and scrap baskets, where it will display its acrobatic powers as it takes coconut, peanuts, hemp and other seeds, meat, fat, suet, pudding and cheese. May help itself to cream off the top of your milk bottle if you leave it too long on the doorstep.

Nests in trees or wall holes or crevices. Also in second-hand nests, or the foundations of larger nests. If no natural sites are available it may use letter-boxes, flower-pots, beehives, and almost any kind of hole. Nest lined with a thick layer of hair or down. 5–11 white eggs, splotched with reddish-brown. End April to June. Incubation, 13–14 days; fledging, about 3 weeks. 1 brood.

Nestbox: Enclosed type, with 1⅛in diameter entrance hole, interior depth at least 5in from hole, floor at least 4 × 4in.

Read: *Birds as Individuals*, Len Howard, Collins, 1952. *Titmice of the British Isles*, J. A. G. Barnes, David & Charles, 1975.

BLUE TIT. *Parus caeruleus*. Resident and generally distributed except in north-west Scotland. Woodland, hedges, gardens.

Forages in trees, hedgerows and around houses. Wheat, nuts, seeds and insects. Damage to buds and ripe fruit outweighed by consumption of insects. Pugnacious, will hold insect prey with its feet and dismember with bill almost like a hawk. Confiding species that will come readily to bird feeding stations for almost anything. Milk-drinker, as great tit.

Nests as great tit. 7–14 white eggs usually spotted with light chestnut. Late April/May. Incubation 13–14 days; fledging, 15–21 days. 1 brood.

Nestbox: Enclosed, with 1in to 1⅛in entrance hole, interior as great tit.

Read: as great tit, above.

COAL TIT. *Parus ater*. Resident and generally distributed. Wooded country and gardens with a preference for conifers. Not so commonly found in orchards and hedgerows.

Forages in trees, especially conifers, for insects and spiders. On ground, for seeds and nuts. Not quite so common at bird tables as great and blue tits, but will take the same foods.

Nests in trees, walls or bank holes close to ground. Moss with thick layer of hair or down and feathers. 7–11 white eggs with reddish-brown spots. Late April and May. Incubation, 17–18 days; fledging, 16 days. Usually 1 brood.

Nestbox: as blue tit.

Read: as great tit, above.

CRESTED TIT. *Parus cristatus*. Resident in a few parts of north-east Scotland only. Pine woods and forests.

Forages mainly on tree trunks for insects, ripe pine cone seeds, berries. Will come to feed at tit-bell and, sometimes, at bird table.

Nests in holes or crevices in old and decayed pine stumps, also in alders and birches, and sometimes in fencing posts. Dead moss lined with hair of deer or hare, sometimes feathers or wool. 5–6 white eggs splotched with chestnut-red. End April/May. Incubation, 14–15 days; fledging, 17–18 days. 1 brood.

Nestbox: Enclosed, 1⅛in to 1½in entrance hole. Interior depth not less than 5in, floor not less than 4 × 4in.

Read: as great tit, above.

MARSH TIT. *Parus palustris*. Resident and widespread in most of England and Wales, but not in Scotland or Ireland. Deciduous woods, hedgerows, thickets and sometimes in gardens, but likes to be near woodland, and not, as might be imagined, marshes.

Forages over trees for insects; on ground for weed seeds, beechmast, berries and sunflower seeds. Comes to bird table and hanging devices for food as blue tit.

Nests in holes in willows, alders, etc, and sometimes in walls. Moss with lining of hair or down. 7–8 white eggs, spotted with red-brown. End April and May. Incubation, 13 days; fledging 16–17 days. Possibly 2 broods.

Nestbox: as blue tit.

Read: as great tit, above.

WILLOW TIT. *Parus atricapillus*. Resident. Fairly frequent in parts of south-east England, scattered locally elsewhere. Marshy or damp woods, hedges and thickets.

Forages over trees and on ground for insects, spiders and berries. Will come to bird table for seeds, peanuts.

Excavates a nest chamber in soft, rotten wood – usually in birch, willow or alder. Pad of down mixed with wood-fibre, some feathers. 8 or 9 white eggs usual, spotted with brown-red. Late April and May. Incubation, 13 days; fledging 17–19 days. Probably 1 brood.

Nestbox: Tit box, as for blue tit, but stuff it full of sawdust so that the willow tit has to excavate a hole. But a far more successful method is to get a rotten silver birch or alder trunk about 6ft long and 4 or 5in diameter and strap it to a convenient tree, allowing the bird to finish the job. Cap the top with polythene so that rain cannot penetrate easily. It seems that the presence of a suitable rotten tree which they can excavate is all that is needed to attract them to breed in an area they visit during winter. Nests are usually between 2 to 5ft high, so place the trunk accordingly. Birch is the preferred site, alder, elder and willow a poor second.

Read: as great tit, above.

LONG-TAILED TIT. *Aegithalos caudatus*. Resident and generally distributed except in very barren districts and islands. Thickets, bushy heaths, coppices and hedgerows. Also woods in winter.

Feeds in trees, sometimes on ground, restlessly searching for insects and seeds. Parties visit gardens and bird tables for suet, pudding, bread crumbs, etc.

Nest in bushes, furze or brambles, sometimes in trees. Large egg-shaped nest of moss woven with cobwebs and hair with a lining of many feathers. Entrance hole near top. 8–12 eggs, sometimes unmarked, sometimes a cap of spots or freckles. March/April. Incubation, 14–18 days; fledging, 15–16 days. Normally 1 brood.

Read: *Titmice of the British Isles*, J. A. G. Barnes, David & Charles, 1975.

NUTHATCH. *Sitta europae*. Resident and fairly common in Wales and southern England. Old trees in woods, parkland and gardens.

Dodges about on tree trunks. Wedges nuts, acorns, beechmast and seeds in crevices, and hacks them open with bill. Also takes insects. Will come freely to bird table and hanging devices for hemp, seeds, nuts, cake, fat, etc. Try jamming a brazil nut into a crevice.

Nests in tree-hole or sometimes in wall-hole. Female fills crevices and reduces entrance hole to desired size with mud. Nest lined with flakes of bark or leaves. 6–11 white eggs spotted with red-brown. End April to June. Incubation, 14–15 days; fledging, about 24 days. Usually 1 brood.

Nestbox: Enclosed, 1¼in to 1½in entrance hole. Interior depth not less than 5in, floor not less than 4 × 4in.

TREE CREEPER. *Certhia familiaris*. Resident and generally distributed. Woodland, parks, gardens with large trees.

Forages unobtrusively for insects over trees. Does not come to bird table, but may indulge in crushed nuts, porridge or suet fat spread in crevices of rough-barked trees, especially Wellingtonia. Has visited peanut feeders.

Nests behind loose bark or cracks on tree trunks or behind ivy. Sometimes in wall or building crevices. Twigs, moss, grass, lined with feathers and bits of wool. Usually 6 white eggs with red-brown spots at big end. End April to June. Incubation, 14–15 days; fledging, 14–15 days. May be second brood.

Nestbox: May come to conventional enclosed type, but a wedge-shaped box has been designed specifically by J. M. D. Mackenzie (see drawing below). Alternatively, secure a loose piece of bark to a tree trunk to provide an artificial crevice.

Wedge - shaped box
for Treecreepers

Nuthatch at nut feeder (*Walter Murray/NHPA*)

WREN. *Troglodytes troglodytes.* Resident and generally distributed. Gardens, thickets, woods, rockbanks. Avoids the centres of large towns.

Lives in a world of cracks and crevices, twigs and woodpiles, hedgebottoms, and the mysterious undergrowth round fallen trees. Active and diligent hunter for insects and spiders. Will take crumbs, but is not a common bird table visitor.

Nests in hedges, holes in trees, banks or buildings. Cock bird makes several nests of moss, grass, leaves, etc, and the hen lines the final choice with feathers. 5–6 eggs, white spotted with brownish-red. Incubation, 14–15 days; fledging, 16–17 days. Usually 2 broods.

Nestbox: May take to one of the standard enclosed types, but is much more likely to find a natural or semi-natural place such as a faggot-pile or creeper-clad wall. Leave a bundle of peasticks or a coil of rope in the corner of a shed.

Read: *The Wren*, Edward A. Armstrong, Collins, 1955.

DIPPER. *Cinclus cinclus.* May occasionally occupy an open-fronted robin-type box.

MISTLE THRUSH (Stormcock). *Turdus viscivorus.* Resident and generally distributed, except in high mountains and treeless districts. Large gardens, orchards, woods.

Feeds mainly on ground, although it likes to sing from the highest point of a tree. Thrives on berries and fruit without conflicting with gardeners' interests. Yew and rowan especially, but also hawthorn, holly, mistletoe, juniper, rose and ivy. All wild fruits except blackberry. Will come to ground station, less freely to bird table for sultanas, currants, and bird pudding. Partial to bird garden life without being particularly friendly to man.

Nests usually in tree fork or on bough. Grasses, moss, etc. Strengthened with earth and lined with fine grasses, the rim ornamented with lichens, bits of wool, feathers, etc. 4 tawny-cream to greenish-blue eggs, splotched with brown and lilac. February to April. Incubation, 13–14 days; fledging, 14–16 days. Frequently 2 broods.

FIELDFARE. *Turdus pilaris.* Winter visitor, generally distributed. Open country, fields and hedges.

Flocks feed in open formation across fields, looking for slugs, spiders, insects. In hedgerows, for berries of hawthorn, holly and rowan, yew, etc. In hard weather will come to ground station or bird table for berries, fruit, seeds, pudding, etc. Breeds in Scandinavia, Central and Eastern Europe and Siberia.

SONG THRUSH. *Turdus ericetorum.* Resident and generally distributed. Parks, woods, hedges, shrubberies and gardens, especially around human habitation.

Forages in open and in undergrowth for worms, slugs and especially snails, which it smashes on 'anvil' stones. Also insects, windfalls, berries and seeds. Will eat soft fruit, but is beneficial on the whole. Somewhat nervous visitor to ground station, not so often on bird table, fond of sultanas, also currants, cheese, fat, apples and scraps.

Nests in hedgerows, bushes, trees, among ivy, occasionally in buildings. Strongly-built of grasses, roots, etc. Stiffened with mud and with a unique lining of rotten wood or dung mixed with saliva and moulded into shape by the hen's breast. 4–5 eggs, blue with greenish tinge, spotted black or red-brown. March to August. Incubation, 13–14 days; fledging, 13–14 days. 2 or 3 broods.

REDWING. *Turdus musicus*. Winter visitor, generally distributed. Open country and open woods.

Feeds in loose flocks in field or woods. Worms, slugs, snails, insects. Hawthorn, holly, rowan, yew berries. In hard weather will come to ground station or bird table for berries, seeds, scraps, fruit, etc.

Breeds in Scandinavia, Eastern Europe and Siberia.

BLACKBIRD. *Turdus merula*. Resident and generally distributed. Woods, hedges, gardens, shrubberies.

Feeds in open and in undergrowth, but never far from cover. Makes surprising amount of noise as it searches among dead leaves. Insects, worms (which it often steals from a song-thrush), fruit, berries and seeds. Will come freely to ground station and to bird table, for sultanas especially, cheese, fat, apples, cake, 'Rice Krispies', berries, seeds.

Nests in hedges, bushes, evergreens and ivy, sometimes in outhouses. Nest like song-thrush, but the mud cup is lined with grasses. 4–5 eggs, bluish-green freckled with red-brown. February (or even earlier) to July. Incubation, 13–14 days; fledging, 13–14 days. 2 or 3 broods.

Nestbox: Tray or open-fronted type, with a floor area 12 × 12in.

Read: *A Study of Blackbirds*, D. W. Snow, Allen and Unwin, 1958.

WHEATEAR. *Oenanthe oenanthe*. Has nested in tin cans and tunnel-type prefabs made of bricks sunk in the shingle at Dungeness bird observatory. Be careful to protect the nestbox from excessive sunshine by piling soil or gravel over any metal used.

REDSTART. *Phoenicurus phoenicurus*. Summer resident, widely distributed but local. Woodlands, parks, bushy commons with old trees, ruins, orchards, well-timbered gardens.

Restless bird, flitting amongst branches or hawking for insects. Might come to bird table for berries, fruit and mincemeat.

Hole-nester, tree or stump, building, walls, outhouses, rocks, quarries. Nest made of grasses, strips of bark, mosses, roots, and lined with hair and feathers. About 6 pale blue eggs. May onwards. Incubation, 14 days; fledging, 14 days. Frequently 2 broods.

Nestbox: Enclosed. Entrance hole 1⅛in to 2in diameter, inside depth not less than 5in from hole, floor not less than 4 × 4in.

Read: *The Redstart*, John Buxton, Collins, 1950.

BLACK REDSTART. *Phoenicurus ochruros*. Passage-migrant and winter visitor, some staying to breed in southern England. Cliffs, large old buildings, indus-

Male Blackbird

Fieldfare

Redwing

Female Blackbird

Song Thrush

Mistle Thrush

Male Greenfinch

Male Siskin

ınnock
edge Sparrow)

Female
House Sparrow

Adult
Robin

RG

Juvenile
Robin

trial premises, rocky and 'waste' ground such as building-sites, dumps or ruins.

Restless bird, in trees, over buildings, and on ground. Hawks for insects. Also takes berries. Although it lives amongst us, it is independent of our food, yet surely it might come to a feeding station for minced meat or berries, especially in hard weather.

Nests in crevices and holes of rocks or buildings, or on rafters, under eaves in outbuildings. Loosely-made of grass, moss, fibre, etc, lined with hair and feathers. 4–6 white eggs. Early April onward. Incubation, 12–13 days; fledging, 16–18 days. 2 broods.

ROBIN. *Erithacus rubecula.* Resident and generally distributed, except in extreme north of Scotland. Gardens, hedgerows, woods with undergrowth.

Feeds freely in open and in undergrowth. Insects, spiders, worms, weed seeds, fruit, berries. Has a flattering relationship with man and will follow the digging spade hopefully. Enthusiastic bird-tabler, very fond of mealworms, will also take seeds, nuts, oats, pudding, etc. Fond of butter and margarine, and is alleged to be able to tell the difference! Unsociable bird, it will endure the close company of its relations at the bird table only in hungry times.

Nests in gardens and hedgerows in bankside hollows, tree holes, walls, amongst creeper, on shelves in outbuildings, often at foot of bush or grassy tuft. Foundation of dead leaves and moss, neatly lined with hair and perhaps a feather or two. 5–6 eggs usually. White with sandy or reddish freckles. Late March onward. Incubation, 13–14 days; fledging, 12–14 days. 2 broods.

Nestbox: Old tin or kettle. Ledge or tray, open-fronted box. Interior floor at least 4 × 4in.

Read: *The Life of the Robin*, David Lack, Witherby, 1965.

BLACKCAP. *Sylvia atricapilla.* Summer resident, frequently winters, local but fairly distributed, except in remote north and west. Open woodland, thickly bushy places, gardens with trees.

Active bird, searching in cover for insects, fruit and berries. Not often on ground. Will come to bird table for a wide range of food, including rolled oats, berries, crumbs and scraps.

Nests in bushes (especially snowberry), hedgerows, evergreens. Stems, roots and grasses, lined with finer grass and hair. 5 eggs, light buff or stone ground, blotched brown and ashy. Mid-May onward. Incubation, 10–11 days; fledging, 10–13 days. Often 2 broods.

CHIFFCHAFF. *Phylloscopus collybita.* Summer resident. Insectivorous bird, may come to bird table for kitchen scraps.

GOLDCREST. *Regulus regulus.* Resident and generally distributed except in remote north-west. Woods, coniferous gardens, hedgerows.

Active and tame bird, which flits from twig to twig searching for spiders and insects. Will come to bird table and to hanging fat.

Nests in thick foliage of conifer. Ball of moss lined with feathers; held together by spiders' webs and suspended from branch. 7–10 white/ochreous eggs, spotted brown. End April to early June. Incubation, about 16 days; fledging, about 18–20 days. 2 broods.

FIRECREST. *Regulus ignicapillus.* Few resident in New Forest, scarce passage migrant along south coast. Woods, gardens, scrub, bracken.

Habits more or less as goldcrest, will occasionally take suet or fat from crevices in tree-bark, etc.

Nests in tree or wall-holes; a loose nest of leaves, bark and mosses, lined with hair and feathers. 5–9 eggs, late May. Incubation 12–13 days; fledging, about 13 days. Single brood.

Nestbox: May use tit box.

SPOTTED FLYCATCHER. *Muscicapa striata.* Summer resident, generally distributed. Gardens, parks, woodland edges.

Sits on an exposed perch, flits out frequently to hawk after flying insects.

Nests against wall or on small ledge supported by creeper or fruit tree, etc. Moss and grass, lined with wool, hair and feathers. 4–5 greenish-grey eggs with brown spots. Mid-May to June. Incubation, 12–13 days; fledging, 12–13 days. 1 brood.

Nestbox: Ledge or open-fronted box with a 3 × 3in floor.

PIED FLYCATCHER. *Muscicapa hypoleuca.* Summer resident locally in parts of Great Britain. Woods, parks, gardens, usually near water.

Catches insects in flight by hawking, but also takes them from trees and on the ground. Worms and berries occasionally.

Nests in holes of trees, walls. Bark, leaves, grasses with a lining of fibres and grass. 4–7 pale blue eggs. Mid-May. Incubation, 12–13 days; fledging, 13 days. 1 brood.

Nestbox: Enclosed. Entrance hole 1⅛in to 2in diameter, inside depth not less than 5in from hole, floor not less than 4 × 4in.

DUNNOCK (Hedge Sparrow). *Prunella modularis.* Resident and generally distributed. Gardens, shrubberies, hedgerows.

Forages unobtrusively on ground among dead leaves, hedgerow bottoms, etc. Weed seeds in winter, insects in summer. Will come freely to ground station, less readily to bird table for crumbs of cornflakes, cake, biscuit, seeds. Unlike most other birds will eat lentils.

Nests in hedges and evergreens, faggot heaps. Twigs, moss, leaves, etc, lined with moss, hair and feathers. 4–5 deep blue eggs. April onward. Incubation, 12 days; fledging, 12 days. 2 broods. Often serves as host to cuckoo.

MEADOW PIPIT. *Anthus pratensis.* Abundant. Open country, moors, heaths, sand dunes, wintering on lowland pastures, sewage-farms, sea coast. Feeds mainly on insects, some weeds. Came to ground food-stations of houses estate-built on reclaimed saltmarsh near Bristol, a traditional wintering place. Early winter the most likely time to see it in the garden.

ROCK PIPIT. *Anthus spinoletta.* Resident and generally distributed. Rocky shores in summer; marshes, waterways, estuaries and coasts in winter.

Forages near water for insects, animals and vegetable matter. Will come freely to a ground feeding station near the shore for crumbs, scraps, cheese.

Nests in hole or cliff-crevice close to the shore. Stems and grasses, lined with grass and hair. 4–5 greyish-white eggs spotted olive-brown and ashy-grey. Late April to June. Incubation, about 14 days; fledging, 16 days. 2 broods.

PIED WAGTAIL. *Motacilla alba.* Resident and generally distributed. Gardens, farms, buildings and cultivated country.

Restless bird, feeds over ground, but often flutters up to take an insect. Mainly insects, fond of shallow pool edges. Will come freely to ground feeding station, scavenging crumbs and scraps where other birds have left unconsidered trifles.

Nests in holes and on ledges of walls, outhouses, creeper, banks and cliffs. Leaves, twigs, stems lined with hair, wool and feathers. 5–6 eggs, greyish or bluish-white, spotted grey-brown and grey. Late April to June. Incubation, 13–14 days; fledging, 14–15 days. 2 broods. Often host to cuckoo.

Nestbox: Ledge or open-fronted box, with a floor area of not less than 16sq in. Fix it in a stone wall; or make a cavity behind a loose stone which can be used as an inspection door.

WAXWING. *Bombycilla garrulus.* Irregular winter visitor, usually to eastern counties. Hedgerow berries. May come to bird table for fruit in hard weather.

STARLING. *Sturnus vulgaris.* Resident and generally distributed. Found almost anywhere, having successfully adapted itself to man's ways.

Active bird, foraging on ground and in trees and hawking for insects. Animal and vegetable foods of almost any kind. Enthusiastic bird table and ground station visitor. Sometimes defeated by hanging devices, but individuals have even learnt to extract peanuts from mesh bags. Very fond of fresh creamy milk and leg-of-lamb bones, particularly marrow, but will eat anything available.

Nests, often in colonies, in tree or building holes. Untidy structure of straw and grasses lined with feathers. 5–7 pale blue eggs. End March onwards. Incubation, 12–13 days; fledging, 20–22 days. 1 brood usually.

Nestbox: Enclosed. Entrance hole 2in diameter, inside depth 12in, floor area 9in by 9in. Starlings will sometimes take over an *old* titbox, when the wood has softened enough to enable them to hack away at the hole and enlarge it.

HAWFINCH. *Coccothraustes coccothraustes.* Resident, generally distributed, but not much in evidence; local in Great Britain, but very rare in Ireland. Woodland, parks, orchards and wooded gardens.

Feeds in trees, taking kernels and seeds. Fond of green peas. Will come shyly to bird table for fruit, seeds and nuts. Highly-developed bill muscles enable it to crack cherry and plum stones, etc, to extract the kernel.

Nests on fruit tree branches or in bushes and other trees. Foundation of twigs supports shallow cup of lichens, moss, grass lined thinly with roots and hair. 4–6 eggs, ground colour light bluish or greyish-green spotted and streaked blackish-brown. Late April onwards. Incubation, 9½ days; fledging, 10–11 days. Occasionally 2 broods.

Read: *The Hawfinch*, Guy Mountfort, Collins, 1957.

GREENFINCH. *Chloris chloris*. Resident and common. Gardens, shrubberies, farmland.

Feeds sociably on ground and in trees. Seeds of all kinds, berries, fruit tree buds, occasionally beetles, ants, aphids. Comes to bird table and seed hoppers for sunflower seed especially, but is most enthusiastic about peanuts. Will appear where not previously seen when peanut bag hoisted. Will even eat buckwheat. Berries of yew, ivy, hawthorn, elder, etc.

Nests in hedgerows and evergreen bushes and trees. Moss interwoven with twigs and lined with roots and hair, sometimes feathers. 4–6 eggs, ground colour dirty white to pale greenish-blue, variably spotted red-brown. Late April/May onwards. Incubation, 13–14 days; fledging, 13–16 days. 2 broods.

Read: *Finches*, Ian Newton, Collins, 1972.

GOLDFINCH. *Carduelis carduelis*. Resident and generally distributed. Gardens, orchards and cultivated land.

Small flocks flitter around plant seed-heads, not so much on the ground. Seeds, especially thistle, teazle and other weeds. Also insects. Will come occasionally to the bird table for small seeds of grains and grasses. Crack some hemp for them, as their beaks are not as strong as those of other finches. Has been known to take peanuts from a string.

Nests especially in fruit trees and chestnuts. Also in hedges and thick berberis. Elegant nest of roots, grass, moss and lichens, lined with vegetable down and wool, placed far out at the end of the branch. 5–6 bluish-white eggs, spotted and streaked red-brown. Early May onwards. Incubation, 12–13 days; fledging, 13–14 days. 2 broods.

SISKIN. *Carduelis spinus*. Resident in parts of Ireland, Scotland and Wales and in Devon, the New Forest and Norfolk. Increasing. Mainly winter visitor, widely distributed. Woods in summer, otherwise copses, streams, gardens.

Seen in mixed parties with redpolls searching spruce, birch and larch for seeds. Since the mid-1960s has become increasingly common in gardens in winter, a habit which spread from Surrey through the south-east. Perhaps first attracted by suitable seed-bearing trees, it has stayed to enjoy the bird table, specialising in meat fat and peanuts. Very tame, seeming almost indifferent to man, though aggressive in behaviour to other birds. Said to be especially attracted to peanuts in *red* mesh bags, but at least one observer found that while red mesh failed, nuts in a *white* RSPB scrap cage did the trick.

Nests in conifers, high up. Moss and wool interwoven with grass and twigs. Lined with rootlets, down and feathers. 3–5 eggs. April–May. Incubation, 11–12 days; fledging about 15 days. 2 broods.

LINNET. *Acanthis cannabina*. Grain-eater, which may come to bird table for kitchen scraps.

REDPOLL. *Acanthis flammea*. Grain-eater, which may come to bird table for kitchen scraps. Especially in Scotland.

BULLFINCH. *Pyrrhula pyrrhula*. Resident and generally distributed. Shrubberies, copses, gardens, orchards, hedgerows.

In autumn and early winter eats mainly weed seeds, some berries; in a hard winter, if its natural food, ashmast, is short it will ravage fruit tree buds. Remedy is to spread 'Transweb' (Transatlantic Plastics Ltd, Ventnor, IoW) among branches of smaller trees and shrubs. Unsightly but effective. Not keen on bird tables, may occasionally come for seeds and berries, but is especially fond of black and red rape. Will take peanuts from a mesh bag (or from another bird), but cannot extract them from shell.

Nests in hedges, evergreen bushes, creeper, brambles. Foundation of twig and moss, cup lined with interlacing roots and hair. 4–5 green-blue eggs with few purple-brown spots and streaks. Late April onwards. Incubation, 12–14 days; fledging, 12–17 days. At least 2 broods.

CROSSBILL. *Loxia curvirostra*. Late summer visitor. Varying numbers. Every few years invades and over-winters in great numbers, many individuals remaining to breed. Coniferous woods, gardens and parks.

Clambers about branches parrot-fashion in parties, wrenching off pine and larch cones. Holds cone in foot while it splits the scales and extracts the seed with its tongue. Apart from cone seeds, will eat thistle seeds, berries and insects. Very tame, it will visit bird table for seeds, especially sunflower. Very fond of water and bathing.

Nests on pine branches. Foundation of twigs, cups of moss, grass and wool lined with grass, fur, hair, feathers. 4 greenish-white eggs with few spots/ streaks of purple-red. January to July. Incubation, 12–13 days; fledging, more than 24 days.

CHAFFINCH. *Fringilla coelebs*. Resident and widely distributed. Gardens, hedgerows, woods, commons, farmland.

Forages on ground and in trees. Insects, spiders, fruit, fruit buds. Tame and enthusiastic bird-tabler, taking seeds of all kinds, bird pudding, scraps and berries.

Nests in hedgerows, orchards, gardens, not choosy. Beautiful structure of moss with interwoven grass and roots, decorated with lichens held together by spiders' webs. Lined with hair and feathers. 4–5 greenish-blue to brownish-stone eggs, spotted/streaked purplish-brown. Mid-April to June. Incubation, 11–13 days; fledging, 13–14 days.

BRAMBLING. *Fringilla montifringilla*. Has been known to take mixed seeds dropped from bird table and peanuts from a mesh bag.

YELLOWHAMMER (Yellow Bunting). *Emberiza citrinella*. Resident and generally distributed. Farmland with hedgerows or bushy cover, bushy commons and heaths. Very common along roadsides.

Feeds mainly on ground, hopping and pecking for corn, weed seeds, wild fruits (including blackberries, which most birds don't like), leaves, grasses. Insects, spiders, worms, etc. Will come to garden seed-hopper once it has discovered it, but not really a garden bird.

Nests in bottom of hedgerow or bush. Straw, grass, stalks, moss-lined with hair and grass. 3–4 eggs, whitish to purplish to brownish-red with dark brown hairlines and spots. Late April to August or later. Incubation, 12–14 days; fledging, 12–13 days. 2 or 3 broods.

REED BUNTING. *Emberiza schoeniclus.* Resident and generally distributed, except in Shetlands. Reed-beds, rushy pastures, marginal land and hedgerows, having expanded recently to add dry country and suburbia to its ancestral wetland habitat.

In wintertime joins with yellowhammers and finches in open fields and visits gardens, often in early spring, for seeds and crushed oats.

Nests in marshy ground, with thick vegetation, sometimes in bushes. Dried grasses and moss, lined with fine grasses, hair. 4–5 eggs, bluish. May/April. Incubation about 13–14 days; fledging, 10–13 days. 2 or 3 broods.

Nestbox: May take advantage of goose/duck raft and nest on it.

SNOW BUNTING. *Plectrophenax nivalis.* Has patronised Scottish bird tables, and vessels of the Royal Navy in northern latitudes.

HOUSE SPARROW. *Passer domesticus.* Resident and widely distributed. Cultivated land and vicinity of human habitation.

Operates in non-territorial 'gangs', cleaning up wherever there are easy pickings on farms, hedgerows, parks, gardens, docks, railways, and 'waste' land of all kinds. Corn, seeds, insects. Tough customer at the bird table, eating almost anything, especially cereal-based foods. Wastes a great deal. Much too successful; where there are too many sparrows other birds tend to get crowded out. Has learned to extract peanuts from net bags, sometimes even hovering to do so. May hang upside-down tit-style to get at nuts from a 'difficult' feeder.

Nests in holes or niches around occupied houses; eaves, drainpiping, creeper, also in hedges and trees, house martins' nests, or in the foundations of rooks' nests. Untidy structure of straw and grasses lined with feathers and oddments. In cramped locations may consist of lining only. 3–5 greyish-white eggs, finely spotted grey and brown. May to August. Incubation, 12–14 days; fledging, 15 days. 2–3 broods.

Nestbox: Enclosed. Entrance hole 1¼in diameter, inside depth not less than 5in, floor 6 × 6in. May easily become a pest, denying nestboxes to more welcome birds. Drastic solution is to destroy nests as soon as they are built.

Read: *The House Sparrow,* J. D. Summers-Smith, Collins, 1963.

TREE SPARROW. *Passer montanus.* Resident and widely-distributed in England and Wales, eastern side of Scotland and a few parts of Ireland. 'Country cousin' of house sparrows, frequenting same habitat but less attached to habitations.

Feeds on weed seeds, corn, insects, spiders. Will visit bird table for seeds and scraps but is a shy bird compared with the house sparrow.

Greenfinch (*L. R. Dawson/Bruce Coleman Ltd*)

Goldfinch (*D. N. Dalton/NHPA*)

Siskin (*S. G. Porter/Bruce Coleman Ltd*)

Great tit (*Eric Hosking*)

Nests in holes of trees, banks, haystacks and thatch, buildings, and in foundations of disused rook or magpie nests. Untidy structure similar to house sparrow. 4–6 eggs, smaller, browner, darker, than house sparrow. Late April to August. Incubation, 12–14 days; fledging, 12–14 days. 2 broods usually.

Nestbox: Enclosed, entrance hole 1⅛in diameter, inside depth not less than 6in, floor not less than 4 × 4in.

One or two surprises!

RING-NECKED PARAKEET (or rose-ringed parakeet). *Psittacula krameri*. This African/Indian species has been colonising the fringes of London since first escaping from captivity (or being deliberately released) around 1969. Now breeding successfully, it may spread. Suburban parks, large gardens. Feeds freely at bird tables. Offer it dates, if you can afford them. Nests in tree holes. Presumably it will take to enclosed boxes.

BUDGERIGAR. *Melopsittacus undulatus*. Escaped or released cage birds sometimes breed in the wild in the south east. There is an established free-flying colony on the island of Tresco, in the Scillies. These birds, often very tame, will come readily to feeding devices for seeds.

CANARY. *Serinus canaria*. As budgerigar, will use seed feeders.

7 Why only birds?

Birds tend to get more than their fair share of attention. Other animals are equally interesting and entertaining, and often equally beneficial to the garden. Take insects, for instance. Most people regard all insects as pests whereas, in fact, only a few hundred out of more than 20,000 British species can reasonably be classified as harmful; by harmful, I mean those that interfere with man's activities, damage crops and so forth. No doubt, the pests themselves would take a different view, and many of the species not only live without encroaching on our lives, but are of great benefit to us. Pollinating bees are an obvious example of how useful insects can be, and a wide variety of flies, beetles, butterflies, moths and wasps also pollinate many flowers. Ladybirds, too, are useful, preying on such harmful insects as aphids and thrips, so if you find a winter colony hibernating in some crevice, leave them in peace. Dragonflies are also useful, eating many other insect species which we regard as harmful. Above all, spiders are useful, eating a great quantity of insects.

Toads are interesting creatures to attract to your garden. Provide a convenient home for one – a hole in a wall, a cavity under a stone or plank – and it may stay with you for years and become a family pet. One naturalist had a toad living under his doorstep for thirty-six years. Toads have a well-developed memory for locality, and though they may forage long distances for food, they will return safely afterwards. They will come out in the daytime in a heavy shower but, normally, they feed in the late evening and early at night. They eat snails, beetles, ants and other insects, caterpillars, woodlice and worms, and will even take snakes and mice.

Bats are much maligned creatures which are much more likely to decimate the flying insects round your house than get tangled in your hair. Their numbers are sadly declining, for various reasons including cave-disturbance, rubbish dumping and ill-advised roof fumigation. So you might care to encourage this harmless and useful beast by putting up special nestboxes (see drawing) or by providing a small access-hole to your loft.

Bat roosting box

Hedgehogs make charming friends and no garden should be without one, although I would never suggest keeping one in captivity. Unless your garden is very large, your hedgehog will want to wander a great deal, but if you provide the right facilities it may use your premises as its base. To my mind, this is the most rewarding of all animal relationships. With a captive animal you can never be quite certain that it is content. A free-living, wild creature which chooses to settle with you will give much deeper pleasure, and provide a never-ending source of interest.

Quite apart from their engaging habits, hedgehogs are positively useful. They eat formidable quantities of slugs, millipedes and caterpillars, but not useful insects such as ladybirds, devil's coach-horse and violet ground-beetles. They even eat adders, on occasion, though I would not classify the adder as a pest.

Hedgehogs can be attracted in much the same way as birds. Food must be put out for them and they must be provided with nestboxes. They are nocturnal creatures, coming out to feed at dusk from late March to November. (In the winter they hibernate.) Put out a saucer of milk, and if it has been turned upside down by the morning you can be reasonably sure that a hedgehog has been at it. (Believing it to be a log, they turn it up to see if there are any tasty insects underneath.) They need to have water, too, but your ground-level bird bath will serve very well. Hedgehogs are also fond of tinned salmon, oranges, and tomatoes, as well as the more obvious kitchen scraps.

A most interesting design for a hedgehog nestbox has been developed by the Henry Doubleday Research Association (see *Hedgehogs and the Gardener,* at the

Young Hedgehog
sketched in August

end of this chapter) and, with permission, I am reproducing the dimensions and details of their hog-kennels. The box should be about 12in by 15in by about 13in high, and made of untreated timber. (Hedgehogs have a keen sense of smell, objecting to both tobacco smoke and artificial preservatives.) To prevent cats getting in, there should be an entrance tunnel a couple of feet long and with a 4½in square section.

It is important that there should be a ventilation shaft, and that air should be able to pass freely through the box; otherwise it will become uncomfortably wet inside. But bear in mind that the hedgehog will probably try to fill the box very full with hay and make sure the ventilation pipe doesn't get blocked. Perhaps the best plan is to make a simple 'baffle' with a fairly tightly rolled piece of chicken wire (see illustration). Fit it firmly so that the hedgehog doesn't dislodge it while he's thrashing about inside. The box needs to be rainproof so cover the roof with a piece of polythene that just overlaps the sides of the box. (Do not seal the box completely with polythene or there will be condensation troubles and the inside of the box will become sodden.)

Cover the whole assembly with at least a foot of earth, so that just the entrance tunnel and feeding hatch are visible. Hedgehogs like to have plenty of dry bedding in their homes, so make some hay or dry leaves available near the box entrance. Put it in a container so that it doesn't get wet and they'll drag it across to the box entrance, leaving some odd bits on the way as evidence.

If there are any hedgehogs in your locality (dead bodies on the road are a certain clue), one will soon discover and adopt your box. Otherwise, you may choose to import one. It is no bad thing to collect hedgehogs found in the road, because they are in danger from passing traffic and you are doing them a good turn by rescuing them. However, this should only be done at times when it is unlikely that you are rescuing a female hedgehog which has a nest of babies somewhere. Unfortunately, there is no easy way of sexing hedgehogs. You are safe enough in taking young ones – up to Spanish orange size – at any time, but adults should only be collected in early spring until mid-May, in August, and again from mid-October. Powder the hedgehog with bug-killer to rid it of its parasites before you release it in your garden. Hedgehogs usually have two lit-

ters a year; the gestation period is somewhere between thirty-one and forty days, and the lactation period about four weeks. The young are born blind, their eyes are open at fourteen days and, when three weeks old, they leave the nest, following mother in Indian file.

With luck your box will be occupied all the year, although hedgehogs won't necessarily raise families in it. During the spring and summer an individual may simply use it as a bedroom during the day. But of course he may well choose to hibernate in it when the time comes. Feed your hogs well in autumn, so that they face the long sleep with good reserves of fat. They may be fairly inactive in October if the weather is cold, but true hibernation starts much later and probably in December. Even after this the hedgehog may well make occasional sallies into the great outdoors. They usually emerge from hibernation in March.

You will soon get to know when the hedgehog comes out to feed and, if you provide a feeding station nearby, you will find that the animal is very tame and will take titbits, especially mealworms, from your hand. Avoid sudden noises, move and talk quietly.

One last warning. If you encourage hedgehogs, or any other animal for that matter, to live in your garden – do not use organo – chlorine garden pesticides of any kind.

Read: *Beneficial Insects*, by B. D. Moreton: Bulletin No 20 of the Min of Ag and Fish: published by HMSO.

Hedgehogs and the Gardener: published by the Henry Doubleday Research Association, Bocking, Braintree, Essex.

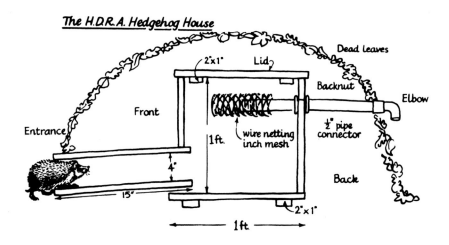

The H.D.R.A. Hedgehog House

Hedgehog feeding from plate of bread and milk (flash photograph) (*B. Alfieri/NHPA*)

Appendices

A Birds which visit feeding stations

Mallard
Canada Goose
Mute Swan
Pheasant
Moorhen
Turnstone
Herring Gull
Black-headed Gull
Wood Pigeon
Collared Dove
(Feral Pigeon)
Kingfisher
Green Woodpecker
Great Spotted Woodpecker
Lesser Spotted Woodpecker
Rook
Jackdaw
Magpie
Jay
Great Tit
Blue Tit
Coal Tit
Marsh Tit
Willow Tit
Long-tailed Tit
Nuthatch

Tree Creeper
Wren
Mistle Thrush
Fieldfare
Song Thrush
Redwing
Blackbird
Robin
Blackcap
Goldcrest
Dunnock
Meadow Pipit
Rock Pipit
Pied Wagtail
Starling
Hawfinch
Greenfinch
Goldfinch
Siskin
Bullfinch
Crossbill
Chaffinch
Yellowhammer
House Sparrow
Tree Sparrow

B Birds which use nestboxes

Regularly
Mallard
Stock Dove
Tawny Owl
Swift
Great Spotted Woodpecker
Wryneck
Jackdaw
Great Tit
Blue Tit
Coal Tit
Marsh Tit
Nuthatch
Redstart
Robin
Spotted Flycatcher
Pied Flycatcher
Starling
House Sparrow
Tree Sparrow

Occasionally
Barn Owl
Little Owl
Green Woodpecker
Swallow
House Martin
Sand Martin
Willow Tit
Tree Creeper
Wren
Blackbird
Pied Wagtail

The British Trust for Ornithology runs a Nest Record Scheme, in which the object is to collect information about the breeding behaviour of British birds. If you feel you could collect simple, but precise, information about the birds which nest in your garden, and not necessarily in nestboxes, write to the BTO, Beech Grove, Tring, Herts, for information.

C Recipes

1 Basic pud
Take seeds, peanuts, cheese, oatmeal, dry cake, and scraps. Put them in a container, pour hot fat over the mixture until it is covered, and leave to set. Turn out onto a table, unless you have prepared it in a tit-bell or coconut holder. Rough quantities: 1lb of mixture to ½lb of melted fat.

2 Bird cake
2lb self-raising flour (Allinsons); ½lb margarine; and a little sugar. Mix with water and bake like large rock bun.

3 Anti-sparrow pudding
Boil together for five minutes one cup of sugar and one cup of water. Mix with one cup of melted fat (suet, bacon or ordinary shortening), and leave to cool.
   Mix with breadcrumbs, flour, bird seed, a little boiled rice and scraps, until the mixture is very stiff. Then pack in any kind of tin can or glass jar. Lay the can on its side in a tree, on the window sill, or in any place where birds can perch and pick out the food. The can must be placed securely, so that the birds cannot dislodge it nor rain get inside. May not fool sparrows for long, though, so don't take it too seriously, or complain to me if it doesn't work.

4 Edwin Cohen's pudding
8oz mutton fat, 12oz coarse oatmeal, 2–3oz flour and 5oz water. Mix flour and oatmeal with liquid fat to stiff paste and bake in shallow pie dish to form flat cakes.

5 Miss Turner's maize cake
Mix maize meal in a bowl with chopped nuts, hemp, canary and millet seed, stir with boiling water till coagulated, then tie tightly in a cloth and leave to dry. Keeps well.

6 Max Knight mix
Stale cake and fat with few dried currants and sultanas. Imprisoned in a 5–8in wire-mesh bag, it keeps birds busy and prevents too much scatter.

SUPPLIERS OF BIRD FOOD
E. W. Coombs Ltd, 25 Frindsbury Rd, Strood, Kent. Sluis Universal Bird Food; meal-worms; seed mixture.
John E. Haith Ltd, Park Street, Cleethorpes, Lincolnshire. Haith's Wild Bird Food; soft-bill food; tit food (in bulk); peanut kernels and shells; sunflower seeds (mixed).
Wholefood Ltd, 112 Baker Street, London W1. Wheat, rye, oats, barley, rice, buck-wheat and millet, whole grain grown organically without the use of chemical pesticides.

SUPPLIERS OF POND PLANTS, etc
Queensborough Fisheries, 111 Goldhawk Road, Shepherds Bush, London W12. Send for list.
The London Aquatic Co Ltd, 42 Finsbury Rd, Wood Green, London N22. Illustrated catalogue.

D Suppliers of bird furniture

Royal Society for the Protection of Birds, The Lodge, Sandy, Bedfordshire. Free catalogue on application. All the RSPB equipment is made of high-quality weather-resistant materials. The woodwork is treated with a harmless preservative and painting is unnecessary. Instructions and advice are included where necessary. All the wooden articles are made in the workshops for the mentally handicapped in Cambridge.

RSPB BIRD TABLE, illustrated overleaf, is 18in by 12in, well proportioned. It may be suspended by chains or fixed on to a 4sq in post. Chains and post socket supplied as standard fitments, but *not* the post. The roof overlaps the table slightly and ensures that food is kept dry in most conditions, although strong winds and driving rain inevitably play havoc. But this is the best buy in bird tables. The roof is fitted with rails to take a food-hopper, which slides into place well sheltered.

HANGING BRACKET, for suspending the table, from a tree, wall or window frame. Strong and rust resistant.

SEED-HOPPER, for dispensing seed mixtures. Fits neatly under bird table roof, for which it is specially made. Hoppers can be very tiresome gadgets, as they are so susceptible to wind and to rain-jamming, but this one is good.

DRINKING TRAY, made in fibreglass with simulated stone finish to harmonise with rockery, or to disguise an unsightly manhole cover. 18in by 14in by 4in overall.

STANDARD NESTBOX, for hole-nesting species with 1⅛in diameter entrance hole to exclude sparrows. Removable top for cleaning. Highly recommended.
Metal entrance-hole protector, which prevents squirrels, woodpeckers, etc, enlarging the hole.

OPEN-FRONT NESTBOX for robins, spotted flycatchers, etc.

SPIRAL TIT FEEDER, with window bracket and suction cup.

TIT FEEDER, more substantial affair, wooden box with wire mesh access to peanuts. 6in by 3½in.

FOOD BASKET, a strong, wire mesh basket, plastic coated for rust prevention, with lid, to take shelled peanuts or scraps. 5½in by 3in.

Nerine Nurseries, Brookend, Welland, Worcestershire. ARTIFICIAL HOUSE MARTIN NESTS, illustrated below, act as a magnet to this species and encourage the establishment of a colony. The nests are fixed under the eaves of house or barn. Sometimes house sparrows may worm their way in by enlarging the holes but Nerine Nurseries supply a leaflet with instructions for a simple anti-sparrow method. Incidentally this method, involving a screen of 12in weighted cords, 2½in apart, and hung 6in away from the entrance hole, can be used to protect natural house martin nests as well.

Richard Dendy, 2 Aultone Yard, Aultone Way, Carshalton, Surrey. Fibreglass birdbath for water or dust, and a fibreglass bird feeder. Send for information.

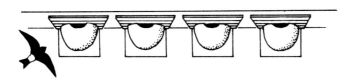

Scottish National Institution for the War Blinded, Linburn, Wilkieston, by Kirknewton, Midlothian.
Wire and wood feeding devices, nestboxes, bird tables and tit bells. Send for illustrated leaflet.
Jamie Wood Products Ltd, Cross Street, Polegate, Sussex. Nestboxes, tit feeders, bird tables, portable hides.
Sutton Parva Nurseries, Heytesbury, Wiltshire.
Dutch nesting baskets for duck.
Hilary Soper, I Above Town, Dartmouth, Devon.
Pottery bird bells, as on page 51.

Warning. Avoid any peanut feeder which involves a flexible coiled-spring system. These are highly dangerous, since a bird may get its feet jammed when another flies away from the feeder causing the spring to contract. And avoid all-in-one nestbox/feeding-tray/water-trough devices. It is asking for trouble to invite birds to eat or drink at the doorstep to another bird's house, creating territorial stresses and strains which don't do anyone any good!

RSPB bird furniture (*RSPB*)

Bird table in winter (*Walter Murray/NHPA*)

E Lifespans of wild birds

The following figures show the *maximum recorded* lifespan in the wild for an individual of each species (to the nearest year); the *average* life expectancy for wild birds is, of course, very short indeed. These are records of the exceptional individual which has managed to survive against all the odds. The figures are available as a result of the international bird-ringing schemes which have been in operation for many years now with the object of learning more about bird numbers and migrations.

If you come across a bird with a ring on its leg, send full details (ring number, date, place, species of bird, whether the bird is freshly dead or not, or if it was alive and subsequently released, and any other relevant information) to the British Trust for Ornithology, Beech Grove, Tring, Hertfordshire. In due course you will be told the place and date of its original ringing.

Pigeon rings should be sent to the Royal National Homing Union, 22 Clarence Street, Gloucester.

Note: The bracketed figures are certainly unrealistic. The species involved have not been ringed in large numbers and the recovery results have yet to reveal a long-lived individual.

Blackbird	12
Blackcap	6
Bullfinch	8
Chaffinch	10
Creeper, Tree	7
Crossbill	(2)
Dove, Collared	8
Dove, Rock	6
Dove, Stock	9
Dunnock	9
Fieldfare	10
Flycatcher, Pied	9
Flycatcher, Spotted	8
Goldcrest	3
Goldfinch	8
Goose, Canada	15
Greenfinch	13
Gull, Black-headed	30
Gull, Herring	24
Hawfinch	(2)
Hoopoe	(2)
Jackdaw	14
Jay	18
Kestrel	16
Kingfisher	4
Magpie	15
Mallard	20
Martin, House	6

Blackbird at nest (*Brian Hawkes/NHPA*)

Swallow at nest with young (*Inigo Everson/Bruce Coleman Ltd*)

F Organisations concerned with bird life

The Royal Society for the Protection of Birds, The Lodge, Sandy, Bedfordshire.

Illustrated journal *Birds*, free to members. Manages a network of bird reserves, organises many exhibitions and meetings, is much concerned with conservation and with the enforcement of the Protection of Birds Act. All bird-watchers should support this admirable and efficient society.

Membership is £3 pa, but write for free gift catalogue, which tells all.

Young Ornithologists' Club, The Lodge, Sandy, Bedfordshire.

Associated with the RSPB, the YOC is the national club for young people (aged 7 to 15) who are interested in birds or want to learn about them. Quarterly magazine, *Bird Life*, nation-wide projects, outings, courses. Kestrel badge. Subscription 60p pa, but write for details.

The British Trust for Ornithology, Beech Grove, Tring, Hertfordshire.

Minimum membership age, fifteen years. Members may take part in organised field studies, ringing and census work. Issues quarterly journal, *Bird Study*, six-weekly *BTO News*, invaluable field guides and other publications. Works closely with RSPB collecting evidence of effects of toxic chemicals. Lending library. All serious bird-watchers should join. (Send for brochure.)

The British Ornithologists' Union, c/o The Bird Room, British Museum (Natural History), Cromwell Road, London, SW7.

Senior bird society in Great Britain; its main object is the advancement of ornithological science on a world scale. Quarterly journal, *The Ibis*.

The Wildfowl Trust, Slimbridge, Gloucestershire.

Illustrated annual report and periodical bulletins; maintains unique collection of swans, ducks and geese from all parts of the world.

The International Council for Bird Preservation (British Section), British Museum (Natural History), Cromwell Road, London, SW7.

Issues annual report, co-ordinates and promotes international bird conservation.

The Henry Doubleday Research Association, 20 Convent Lane, Bocking, Braintree, Essex.

Issues newsletters and occasional publications of interest to the bird gardener. Initiates research into organic farming and gardening methods; pest control without poisons.

OTHER IMPORTANT SOCIETIES CONCERNED WITH ALL ASPECTS OF NATURAL HISTORY

International Union for Conservation of Nature and Natural Resources, 1110 Morges, Switzerland.

Independent international body promoting and supporting action which will ensure the perpetuation of wild nature and renewable natural resources all over the world.

The World Wildlife Fund, 7–8 Plumtree Court, London EC4.

Raises funds and allocates them to projects covering a wide range from land purchase for national parks and reserves to ecological surveys and emergency programmes for the safeguarding of endangered plants and animals.

The Fauna Preservation Society, c/o The Zoological Society of London, Regent's Park, London NW1.

PERIODICALS

British Birds, published monthly by Macmillan Journals Ltd. A bird-watchers' journal; not too scientific, not too 'pop'; includes monthly report on migrants and rarities.

G Birds and the law

With certain exceptions, all wild birds, their nests and eggs, are protected by law. Under certain provisions of the Protection of Birds Act, 1954, persons guilty of an offence under the Act may be liable to a fine of up to £25 and/or one month's imprisonment in respect of each offence.

Although the present Act, in repealing fifteen previous ones, represents a considerable simplification of the situation that existed before 1954, it is still by no means easy for a layman to understand. If you believe the law to have been broken, make detailed notes of the occurrence and call the police and RSPCA.

The Royal Society for the Protection of Birds has published a free leaflet which explains the Act in plain language. These are some of the questions they are most often asked, with their answers:

What birds are protected in Britain?
With a few exceptions, all birds, their nests and eggs are protected by law and anyone breaking this law is liable to a fine or imprisonment. The main exceptions are certain game birds and species classed as pests.

Is it against the law to collect birds' eggs?
Yes, with very few exceptions. The taking of just one egg of a common bird such as a blackbird or robin could result in a fine of £5.

What about eggs from a deserted nest?
This is also illegal, for the reasons that it prevents someone taking eggs from a nest which he mistakenly believes is deserted, and prevents an unscrupulous person taking eggs from an occupied nest and saying that it had been deserted.

I have found a young boy collecting eggs, should I report him to the police?
No. It would be much better to explain to him why, as well as being illegal, egg collecting is rather pointless and selfish. Try to interest him in watching birds instead – tell him about our Young Ornithologists' Club and the many activities which the club organises for young people.

Can I sell a collection of birds' eggs?
Only by obtaining a licence from the Home Office. Otherwise, the sale and exchange of birds' eggs is illegal.

What can I do about youths who shoot at birds with air guns in our local park?
Inform the police immediately. With few exceptions it is illegal to shoot at any birds and also the youths would be breaking the law by using an air gun in a public place.

A farmer near us is shooting hundreds of wood pigeons, rooks and crows on his land. How can I stop him?
You cannot. These birds are among the species classed as agricultural pests and the owner or occupier of the land is allowed to shoot them.

I would like to have a tame kestrel. Can I take a young one from its nest and rear it myself?
No. It is illegal and more important, unkind. It is also extremely difficult to rear a young bird – its parents can do a far better job.

Is it legal to photograph birds at the nest?
It is now illegal to disturb on or near a nest, by photography or otherwise, birds which are included in the First Schedule of the Protection of Birds Acts (about sixty of the more rare species) without a special licence from the Natural Environment Research

Council. Although it is legal to photograph nesting birds of common species, even this should only be done by a really skilled photographer using the correct equipment – otherwise the birds may desert. Instead, try photographing birds at bird tables, bathing places, etc.

I want to ring birds. How do I start?

You may only ring birds if you have a licence issued by NERC. You may only use official numbered rings, which are issued by the British Trust for Ornithology, if you have a BTO permit; to obtain a BTO permit, you must have been fully trained by a BTO licensed ringer.

I want to put colour rings on some birds in my garden. Where can I buy these rings?

It is illegal even to colour-ring birds. Special licences are only granted to properly qualified ringers by NERC.

Is it legal to keep in captivity a sick or injured bird?

Yes, provided that you release it as soon as it is well and able to fend for itself. The law also allows one to kill a bird which is so seriously injured, other than by one's own action, that it has no reasonable chance of recovery.

Read: '*The Protection of Birds Act; Statutory Instruments,*, HMSO, Kingsway, London WC2.

Wild Birds and the Law (simplified version of the Act), RSPB, The Lodge, Sandy, Bedfordshire. Free leaflet.

H Treatment of casualties

1 *Orphaned or exhausted birds.* First of all, be sure the bird is really in need of help. Youngsters of some species leave the nest before they are really able to fly and hang around in hedge bottoms and in odd corners waiting to be fed. This is perfectly normal and you should leave the birds to get on with the job. Every year, hundreds of unfortunate baby blackbirds and tawny owls get 'rescued' before they are lost.

If you know definitely that the bird is not being fed, then you may decide to act as foster-parent. This can be a long and tedious job, especially in the case of a very young bird. Be very sure that you are prepared to devote a great deal of time and patience to the job before you begin. If you're not absolutely certain you can see it through then the humane action is to kill the bird. Don't condemn it to a few days or weeks of misery before it dies. Large birds may be killed by a heavy blow on the base of the skull, and smaller birds may be killed by breaking their necks as in killing poultry. As well as time and patience you will need a suitable place to keep the patient. Keep it in a warm and draught-free place. Feed with a mixture of swatted-fly, small smooth green caterpillars (not hairy ones), and finely minced raw meat from the end of a matchstick. (Birds of prey must also have roughage, dead mice with the fur still on, for instance.) Handle the bird very gently. Do not feed live food – always kill insects before offering them. Feed once every hour and make sure the crop is full (you can see the food stockpile and swell at the base of the throat).

It is difficult to overfeed a young bird, and it will tell you in no uncertain fashion when it is hungry. Give it water, although it may not drink. Do not 'pet' it; warmth and a cosy 'nest' will substitute for its mother. Keep its nest clean and dispose of its droppings promptly. As it gets older, encourage it to fly to you for food. Then take it into the garden and help it to fend for itself by planting caterpillars, etc and 'discovering' them with it. The bird should be independent of you within a month.

An adult bird is certainly in need of help *if you can pick it up*. An exhausted or starved adult should be put in a box with a carpet of newspaper and a perch-stick low down across the floor. The top should be darkened as birds tend to fly upwards in the light and may stun or kill themselves. Give it a shallow bowl of water and a shallow bowl of food. Budgerigar mixture for seed-eaters; insects, chopped worms, caterpillars, supplemented with packet 'insectivorous' food from a pet shop for insect-eaters. (Soaked bread may be used for a first emergency feed, but *no* alcohol.) Leave it undisturbed in the warm (up to 70°F). Put a light on for a few hours; this will stimulate it to feed. If the bird is still alive next day you can either let it go or continue treatment, depending on how lively it is. But remember the shorter its time in captivity the better.

2 *Injured birds*. These should be taken to the nearest vet, RSPCA or PDSA establishment. Only if you are prevented by some powerful reason from taking this course should you attempt to treat the bird yourself.

Read: *Bird Doctor*, Katherine Tottenham, Nelson; and *Treatment of Sick and Wounded Birds*, F. B. Lake, British Trust for Ornithology, Beech Grove, Tring, Hertfordshire.

Song thrush (*Walter Murray/NHPA*)

Young blue tits bathing (*Walter Murray/NHPA*)

Nobody loves me (*Jane Burton/Bruce Coleman Ltd*)

Bibliography

ANON (1969). *Wildfowl Management;* Eley Game Advisory Station, Fordingbridge, Hampshire.

ANON (1971). *Nest Records Scheme;* BTO, Tring, Herts.

ATKINSON-WILLES, G. L. (1963). *Wildfowl in Great Britain;* HMSO.

BANNERMAN, D. A. (1953–1963). *The Birds of the British Isles;* Oliver & Boyd Ltd.

BATTEN, H. M. (1933). *How to Feed and Attract the Wild Birds;* The Moray Press.

BLOTZHEIM, U. G. VON (1965). Longevity Records of Swiss Birds, *The Ring, 42:* 104–6.

BOSWALL, J. H. R. (1964). A discography of Palearctic bird sound recordings; Witherby.

CAMPBELL, B. (1952). *Bird-Watching for Beginners;* Penguin Books.

——(1953). *Finding Nests;* Collins.

CLEGG, J. (1965). *The Observers' Book of Pond Life;* Warne.

DENNIS, E. (ed) (1972). *Everyman's Nature Reserve;* David & Charles.

DRABBLE, P. (1964). *The Penguin Book of Pets;* Penguin Books.

EADES, R. (1970). *An artificial raft as nesting site;* Seabird Group, Aberdeen University.

FLEGG, J. J. M. and GLUE, D. E. (1974). *Nestboxes;* BTO, Tring, Herts.

FISHER, J. (1940). *Watching Birds;* Penguin Books.

FISHER, J. and LOCKLEY, R. M. (1954). *Seabirds;* Collins.

FISHER, J. and PETERSON, R. T. (1964). *The World of Birds;* Macdonald.

FITTER, R. S. R. (1959). *The Pocket Guide to Nests and Eggs;* Collins.

FLOWER, S. S. (1938). Further Notes on the Duration of Life in Animals, IV. Birds. *Proc Zool Soc Lond 108 (Ser A)* 195–235.

FULLER-MAITLAND, E. (1927). *Small Bird Sanctuaries;* RSPB.

HARTLEY, P. H. T. (1957). *The Bird Garden;* RSPB.

HIESEMANN, M. (English edn 1908). *How to Attract and Protect Wild Birds;* Witherby.

HILLS, L. D. (1964). *Pest Control Without Poisons;* Henry Doubleday Research Assoc.

——(1965). *Hedgehogs and the Gardener;* HDRA.

HOLLOM, P. A. D. (rev edn 1968). *The Popular Handbook of British Birds;* Witherby.
HOWARD, L. (1952). *Birds as Individuals;* Collins.
HUDSON, R. (ed) (1971). *A Species List of British and Irish birds;* BTO, Tring, Herts.
KINNE, R. (1962). *The Complete Book of Nature Photography;* New York.
KNIGHT, M. (1954). *Bird Gardening;* Routledge & Kegan Paul.
MASSINGHAM, H. J. (1924). *Sanctuaries for Birds;* Bell.
MORETON, B. E. (1958). Beneficial Insects. *Min of Ag Bull 20;* HMSO.
NEWTON, I. (1972). *Finches;* Collins.
NICHOLSON, E. M. (1951). *Birds and Men;* Collins.
PETERSON, R. T., MOUNTFORT, G. and HOLLOM, P. A. D. (rev edn 1966). *A Field Guide to the Birds of Britain and Europe;* Collins.
RUDD, R. L. (1965). *Pesticides and the Living Landscape;* Univ of Wisconsin Press.
RYDZEWSKI, W. (1962). Longevity of ringed birds; *The Ring, 33;* 147–52.
SMITH, M. (1951). *British Amphibians and Reptiles;* Collins.
SOPER, T. (1972). *The Shell Book of Beachcombing;* David & Charles.
———(1975). *Wildlife Begins at Home;* David & Charles.
———(1976). *Everyday Birds;* David & Charles.
SOUTHERN, H. N. (ed) (1964). *The Handbook of British Mammals;* Blackwell.
SPARKS, J. (1972). *Animal Design;* BBC Publications.
SPARKS, J. and SOPER, T. (1970). *Owls;* David & Charles.
THOMSON, A. L. (ed) (1964). *A New Dictionary of Birds;* Nelson.
TOTTENHAM, K. (1963). *The Pan Book of Home Pets;* Pan Books.
TURNER, E. L. (1935). *Every Garden a Bird Sanctuary;* Witherby.
TWEEDIE, M. (1968). *Pleasure from Insects;* David & Charles.
VEDEL, H. and LANGE, J. (1960). *Trees and Bushes;* Methuen.
WITHERBY, H. F., *et al* (rev edn 1952). *The Handbook of British Birds* (5 vols); Witherby.

Acknowledgements

Spring 1965

My grateful thanks go to Mary Blair, Tom Edridge, Elaine and H. G. Hurrell, R. M. Lockley, Winwood Reade and E. H. Ware for ploughing through the first draft of this book and offering so much useful advice. David St John Thomas encouraged me to start; hundreds of BBC Spotlight viewers in the West Country forced me to continue by asking questions, instead of answering them as I had requested. Chris Mead and David Wilson of the British Trust for Ornithology and Frank Hamilton and John Taunton of the Royal Society for the Protection of Birds have been most helpful. Many friends have encouraged me with good ideas and corrections; some have even valiantly tried to improve my grammar, but the mistakes that remain are all my own work.

T.S.

Spring 1973

Since this book was first published, I have had a considerable correspondence with readers who have corrected and improved the information in it, and asked yet more questions. My sincere thanks to them; I think I have incorporated all the new material in this edition. But it is clear that no bird gardening book will ever be complete. So I throw in my hand again with a mixture of pleasure and trepidation.

T.S.

Spring 1977

At last . . . in colour! My thanks to all correspondents, even those who telephone in the middle of Dr Who. Also thanks to Robert Gillmor for his superb drawings and his enviable facility for doing them at the speed of flight, at least when pressure is firmly applied. And to Chris Mead and David Glue of the BTO, who combine scientific standards with an understanding of the enthusiasms of mere pleasure-bird-watchers. And to people like Mr and Mrs Pat Willson who run the BTO's Garden Bird Feeding Survey, which collects and collates the hard facts. And to Pam Thomas of David & Charles, who makes publishing books fun. I tremble at the thought of what must surely come next — The Bird Table Book in 3D. Watch this space!

T.S.
Above Town
Dartmouth
Devon

Blue tit (*John Markham/Bruce Coleman Ltd*)

Index

References to photographs or drawings are printed in italics. The main entry for a bird in the 'species notes' section is in bold type.

If you would happy company win,
Dangle a palm-nut from a tree, idly in greed to sway and spin,
Its snow-pulped kernel for bait; and see
A nimble titmouse enter in.

Titmouse Walter de la Mare.

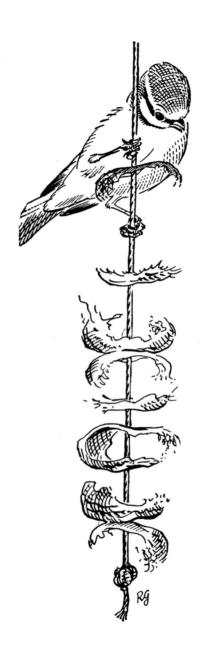